# PORTLAND YOUR WAY

A Guide for Every Traveler, Style, and Season in Portland, Maine

## TRAVEL SERIES
### BOOK 4

## KIMBERLY BURK CORDOVA

# TABLE OF CONTENTS

# INTRODUCTION

## WELCOME TO PORTLAND: A COASTAL GEM

Nestled on Maine's rugged coastline, Portland is a city that lures you in with its charm and leaves you planning your next visit before you've even left. Picture this: cobblestone streets winding through a historic harbor, the salty tang of the Atlantic breeze mingling with the aroma of freshly baked bread wafting from a nearby bakery. Overhead, the cries of seagulls echo above colorful fishing boats docked in the harbor while locals sip coffee at bustling cafés, their laughter spilling into the streets. Portland is a place where the past dances effortlessly with the present, creating a unique blend of tradition, creativity, and community.

What makes Portland special isn't just its postcard-perfect looks—it's the stories woven into every corner. From its beginnings as a maritime powerhouse to its evolution into one of America's most celebrated foodie and cultural destinations, this city offers something for every traveler. Whether you're an art lover, a history buff, or simply someone in search of the perfect lobster roll, Portland promises unforgettable experiences.

## HISTORICAL AND MODERN SIGNIFICANCE: FROM SHIPS TO STARTUPS

Portland's story is one of resilience and reinvention. Long before it became the vibrant hub we know today, the area was home to the Wabanaki people, who called it Machigonne, or "great neck." The city's strategic coastal location made it a vital center for trade, fishing, and shipbuilding during the colonial era. By the 18th century, Portland was thriving, its deep harbor bustling with schooners destined for far-off shores.

But Portland's journey hasn't been without challenges. During the Revolutionary War, British forces bombarded the town, destroying much of its infrastructure. Then came the Great Fire of 1866, a catastrophic blaze that wiped out a third of the city. Yet, each setback only seemed to strengthen Portland's resolve. The town rebuilt itself with remarkable determination, replacing wooden structures with brick and granite, giving birth to the iconic architecture that still defines the Old Port today.

In the 20th century, Portland faced another transformation. As traditional industries like fishing and shipbuilding declined, the city turned its attention to art, culture, and innovation. Today, Portland is a thriving cultural hub, celebrated for its art galleries, award-winning restaurants, and burgeoning tech scene, which has positioned it as one of the Northeast's most dynamic small cities. Despite its modern strides, Portland remains deeply connected to its past, a place where every street tells a story.

## WHY PORTLAND ATTRACTS DIVERSE TRAVELERS: A CITY FOR EVERYONE

Few places can match Portland's ability to cater to such a wide range of interests. It's a city that wears many hats, welcoming families, solo adventurers, couples, and groups alike. Here's what draws travelers from all walks of life:

- **For Families:** Portland offers a perfect mix of education and entertainment. Imagine a day that starts at the Maine

Children's Museum, where interactive exhibits spark curiosity, and ends with a picnic on the Eastern Promenade, overlooking the harbor.

- **For History Buffs:** Walking tours of Portland's historic landmarks, like the Portland Observatory or Victoria Mansion, bring the city's rich past to life.
- **For Foodies:** Portland's culinary scene is second to none, with its farm-to-table ethos, world-class seafood, and craft breweries that make it a gastronomic paradise.
- **For Nature Lovers:** Whether it's kayaking in Casco Bay, hiking in nearby forests, or simply watching the sun set behind Portland Head Light, outdoor enthusiasts will find their sanctuary here.
- **For Art and Culture Seekers:** The city's vibrant arts district offers everything from contemporary galleries to live performances, while its annual festivals celebrate everything from film to food.

Portland's magic lies in its ability to feel both bustling and intimate. It's a place where you can lose yourself in the energy of a festival one moment and find peace in a quiet park the next.

## WHY PORTLAND? A CITY OF CULINARY AND COASTAL TREASURES

Portland's appeal goes beyond its scenery and history. The city is a feast for the senses, offering unparalleled culinary experiences and outdoor adventures that keep visitors coming back for more.

- **The Foodie Scene:** Portland's reputation as a culinary hotspot is well deserved. Whether it's indulging in a buttery lobster roll at a seaside shack or savoring an intricately plated dish at a Michelin-starred restaurant, Portland's food scene caters to every palate. Don't miss the city's vibrant food truck culture, where local chefs serve up everything from wood-fired pizza to gourmet tacos.

- **Outdoor Adventures:** Portland's natural beauty is its playground. Spend your day kayaking through the Casco Bay islands, cycling along the Back Cove Trail, or exploring the serene paths of Mackworth Island. Enjoy sledding or snowshoeing in the winter, followed by a hot cocoa in one of the city's cozy cafés.
- **Inclusivity and Community:** What sets Portland apart is its inclusivity. This is a city where everyone is welcome, from LGBTQ+ travelers to remote workers looking for a creative hub. Portland's warm, welcoming atmosphere makes it more than just a destination—it's a place to belong.

## HOW TO USE THIS GUIDE: TAILORING YOUR ADVENTURE

This guide is designed with you in mind. Whether you're planning a whirlwind weekend or a leisurely weeklong escape, you'll find tips and itineraries tailored to your travel style, budget, and interests.

Here's how to navigate the book:

- **Pick Your Chapter:** Each chapter focuses on a specific aspect of Portland, from its historic neighborhoods to its seasonal highlights. Start with what excites you most.
- **Follow the Icons:** Look out for symbols indicating family-friendly activities, budget tips, and hidden gems to help you make the most of your time.
- **Customize Your Trip:** With Portland's diversity of experiences, this guide gives you the tools to plan your ideal getaway, whether that's hiking coastal trails, sampling craft beers, or exploring art galleries.

## EXPLANATION OF TRAVELER SEGMENTS AND STRUCTURE

To make planning even easier, this guide is divided into traveler-focused sections. Whether you're a foodie, history lover, or luxury traveler, there's something here for you:

- **For the Foodies:** Dive into the culinary treasures of Portland, from lobster rolls to craft beer trails.
- **For the History Buffs:** Explore Portland's maritime legacy and iconic landmarks.
- **For Families:** Discover kid-friendly attractions, educational experiences, and casual dining options.
- **For Budget Travelers:** Get tips on free or low-cost activities and affordable accommodations.
- **For Luxury Travelers:** Uncover upscale dining, boutique hotels, and exclusive experiences.
- **For Outdoor Enthusiasts:** Find the best parks, hiking trails, and water activities.

Each chapter provides detailed recommendations, practical tips, and insider insights to help you craft a trip that matches your style. The goal? To make your Portland adventure as seamless and memorable as possible.

## CLOSING REFLECTION

Portland is a city that defies expectations—a place where history and innovation walk hand in hand, where natural beauty meets culinary brilliance, and where every traveler can find their own version of perfection. As you dive into this guide, let Portland inspire you, surprise you, and welcome you with open arms. Your adventure starts here.

# PART 1: GETTING TO KNOW PORTLAND

1

# THE HEART OF NEW ENGLAND

## A CITY BORN OF SALT AND SEA

Imagine a morning in 18th-century Portland: the salty tang of the Atlantic fills the air as shipbuilders hammer away on massive schooners, their work resonating along the bustling waterfront. Fishermen call out the day's catch, and merchants haggle over barrels of salted cod destined for Caribbean markets. Portland, Maine, has always been defined by the rhythm of its working waterfront, a lifeline to the world and the foundation of its rich history. From its humble beginnings as a fishing village to its current status as a vibrant cultural hub, Portland's story is steeped in resilience, reinvention, and a deep connection to the sea.

## MARITIME HISTORY: SHIPBUILDING, FISHING, AND TRADE

Portland's maritime history begins with its geography. Perched on the Casco Bay, the city boasts a deep, ice-free harbor that has been a beacon for maritime industries since the 17th century. Early settlers recognized its strategic importance, turning the harbor into a bustling center for fishing and shipbuilding.

By the 18th century, Portland was producing some of the finest ships in New England. These wooden vessels, built by skilled craftsmen, carried goods and people across the Atlantic and beyond. The city's shipyards hummed with activity, their products becoming vital links in global trade networks. Fishing was equally essential, with Portland's fleets hauling in abundant catches of cod, herring, and lobster to supply markets as far away as Europe.

Trade made Portland a vital hub in the Atlantic economy. The city's docks buzzed with activity as merchants loaded ships with Maine's prized timber, granite, and salted fish. Returning vessels brought molasses, rum, and other exotic goods, creating a lively waterfront culture where sailors swapped stories and local taverns thrived.

This connection to the sea didn't just shape Portland's economy—it shaped its identity. The waterfront became the city's lifeblood, a place where fortunes were made and traditions were forged. Today, you can still see echoes of this maritime legacy in the working wharves of the Old Port and the fishing boats moored in the harbor.

## HOW PORTLAND EVOLVED INTO A MODERN CULTURAL HUB

Portland has never been a city to rest on its laurels. Over the centuries, it has reinvented itself time and again, weathering fires, wars, and economic upheavals with a determination that defines its character.

One of the most pivotal moments in Portland's history was the Great Fire of 1866, a devastating blaze that destroyed more than 1,500 buildings and left much of the city in ruins. For many towns, such a catastrophe would have spelled disaster. But Portland's residents saw it as an opportunity to rebuild—and rebuild they did, using brick and granite to create the iconic architecture that defines the Old Port today.

As the 20th century dawned, Portland faced new challenges. Traditional industries like fishing and shipbuilding began to decline, leaving the city at an economic crossroads. Rather than fading into obscurity, Portland reinvented itself as a hub for culture, creativity, and innovation. The Arts District emerged as a centerpiece of this transformation, attracting artists, musicians, and entrepreneurs who breathed new life into the city.

Today, Portland is a cultural powerhouse. Its vibrant neighborhoods are filled with galleries, theaters, and live music venues. Its restaurants, many of which embrace a farm-to-table ethos, have earned it a reputation as one of America's top culinary destinations. And its breweries, wineries, and distilleries have turned Portland into a mecca for craft beverage enthusiasts.

This evolution didn't happen overnight. It's the result of a community that values both its history and its future, a city that has found a way to honor its past while embracing the possibilities of tomorrow.

## MAJOR HISTORICAL MILESTONES SHAPING THE CITY

Portland's history is marked by moments of profound change—turning points that have defined its character and charted its course. Here are some of the key milestones that have shaped the city:

- **The Founding of Falmouth (1632):** Before it was Portland, the area was part of the town of Falmouth, a settlement that grew around the fishing and trading industries. Its harbor made it a critical hub for maritime commerce, laying the foundation for what would become one of New England's most important cities.
- **British Bombardment (1775):** During the Revolutionary War, British forces attacked Falmouth, burning much of the town to the ground. This devastating event rallied local support for independence and cemented Portland's reputation for resilience.
- **The Great Fire of 1866:** Sparked by a careless Fourth of July celebration, this inferno destroyed a third of the city, including much of the Old Port. The fire spurred a wave of rebuilding, transforming Portland into a city of brick and granite that could withstand the challenges of the future.

- **The Prohibition Era (1920s):** Maine was the first state to enact Prohibition, and Portland became a hotspot for bootlegging and speakeasies. This rebellious spirit lives on in the city's craft beverage scene, which celebrates creativity and innovation.
- **The Rise of the Arts District (1990s):** As the city reinvented itself in the late 20th century, the Arts District became a focal point for Portland's cultural renaissance. Today, it's home to the Portland Museum of Art, the State Theatre, and countless galleries and studios.
- **Economic Revitalization (21st Century):** With its thriving tourism industry, burgeoning tech startups, and commitment to sustainability, Portland has entered a new era of prosperity. Once a gritty working waterfront, the Old Port is now a vibrant area filled with shops, restaurants, and nightlife.

## WHERE THE PAST MEETS THE PRESENT

Portland's history is a tale of resilience, reinvention, and relentless determination. Its journey from a humble fishing village to a modern cultural hub is a testament to the spirit of its people and the power of community. But Portland isn't just a city defined by its history—it's a city shaped by its neighborhoods. In the next chapter, we'll take a closer look at the places that make Portland unique, from the Old Port's cobblestone charm to the Arts District's artistic energy.

（２）

# NEIGHBORHOODS OF PORTLAND

## A NEIGHBORHOOD FOR EVERY MOOD

Portland isn't just a city—it's a collection of distinct neighborhoods, each with its own personality, stories, and quirks. Living in Portland feels like being part of a small-town community nestled within the charm of a historic city. Whether you're wandering cobblestone streets in the Old Port, exploring the cultural pulse of the Arts District, or savoring the quiet elegance of the West End, every corner of this city offers a sense of belonging. For me, Portland wasn't just home—it was a constant discovery of new flavors, experiences, and stories waiting to be shared.

## OLD PORT: COBBLESTONE STREETS AND WATERFRONT CHARM

The Old Port is the beating heart of Portland, its cobblestone streets and brick buildings evoking a timeless charm. It's a neighborhood that seems almost designed for wandering—ducking into hidden shops, grabbing a coffee, or pausing to watch the fishing boats bobbing in the harbor. Living in Portland, this was one of my favorite areas to stroll through with my daughter Channa. Together, we'd pop into little boutiques and consignment shops, marveling at how these historic storefronts housed everything from handmade jewelry to local art.

The Old Port has always had a unique energy. Even during the quieter days of the COVID-19 pandemic, it was the soul of the city. Channa, her husband Stephen, and I made it a point to order takeout from some of our favorite spots in the area to help these small restaurants survive. We'd savor lobster rolls from **Eventide Oyster Co.** (86 Middle St, Portland, ME | +1 207-774-8538) or gourmet burgers from **Duckfat** (43 Middle St, Portland, ME | +1 207-774-8080) at home, reminding ourselves that the lack of chain restaurants in Portland is what gives the city its unique flavor—literally and figuratively.

What makes the Old Port truly special is its stories. This is where tunnels beneath the streets were once used by smugglers during Prohibition and where the Great Fire of 1866 began, forever reshaping Portland's architecture. Walking these streets feels like stepping into history, where every brick has a story to tell.

## ARTS DISTRICT: PORTLAND'S CREATIVE SOUL

The Arts District always struck me as a place where creativity thrives, and imagination finds a home. Walking along Congress Street, you can feel the pulse of Portland's artistic energy. Murals pop from the walls, galleries invite exploration, and the theaters brim with performances that stir your soul.

When my daughter and I weren't indulging our love for good food, we'd often find ourselves drawn to this area, taking in the rotating exhibits at the **Portland Museum of Art** (7 Congress Square, Portland, ME | +1 207-775-6148) or browsing the eclectic offerings at First Friday Art Walks. The creativity here is infectious—you can't help but leave inspired.

One of my favorite memories of the Arts District was discovering **SPACE Gallery** (538 Congress St, Portland, ME | +1 207-828-5600) for the first time. Its edgy and experimental vibe was unlike anything else in the city, and it became one of those places that reminded me why Portland felt so alive. It wasn't just about the art—it was about how the community embraced it, celebrating creativity in all its forms.

## MUNJOY HILL: RESIDENTIAL CHARM AND PANORAMIC VIEWS

Munjoy Hill always felt like an escape—a place where the city's bustle melted away, and the views took your breath away. Walking along the Eastern Promenade was a ritual, especially when I needed a moment of peace. The sweeping views of Casco Bay, with its islands dotting the horizon, made you feel like you were standing at the edge of the world.

The history of Munjoy Hill is palpable, from the Civil War encampments to the enduring presence of the **Portland Observatory** (138 Congress St, Portland, ME | +1 207-774-5561). Visiting the observatory with Channa felt like stepping back in time, imagining the sailors and merchants who once relied on this signal tower to navigate the city's busy harbor. It was in these moments that Portland's layers of history felt so tangible.

Munjoy Hill also held some of our favorite hidden culinary gems. Whether it was grabbing coffee from **Hilltop Coffee** (100 Congress St, Portland, ME | +1 207-780-7700) or dining at **The Blue Spoon** (89 Congress St, Portland, ME | +1 207-773-1116), the neighborhood's small businesses always felt personal—like every cup of coffee or plate of food came with a side of Portland's welcoming spirit.

## WEST END: VICTORIAN ELEGANCE AND SERENE GREEN SPACES

The West End was my home in Portland, and it remains my favorite neighborhood in the city. I lived in what was once the neighborhood's only elementary school, a building converted into condominiums in the 1980s. Every time I walked through the cobblestone streets, I was struck by the Victorian charm of the area. It felt like stepping back in time, with each house a piece of living history.

I loved exploring the West End with Channa, often stopping at consignment stores to hunt for unique finds. The neighborhood's peaceful streets and historic character made it the perfect backdrop for these small adventures. One of our favorite spots was **Victoria Mansion** (109 Danforth St, Portland, ME | +1 207-772-4841), an architectural gem that felt like Portland's version of a time capsule.

The West End also held some of our most cherished dining experiences. The James Beard award-winning cuisine of Portland often brought us to restaurants like **Chaval** (58 Pine St, Portland, ME | +1 207-772-1110), where the seasonal menu always felt like an invitation to explore new flavors. The fact that Portland's food scene thrived on local, independent businesses was something we cherished deeply—especially during COVID when supporting those small restaurants felt like supporting the heartbeat of the city.

## SOUTH PORTLAND: COASTAL ESCAPES AND ICONIC LANDMARKS

While I lived on the Portland peninsula, South Portland always felt like a perfect day-trip destination—a place where you could escape the city's rhythm and embrace the serenity of the coast. Willard Beach was a favorite spot for quiet walks; its calm waters and sandy shores a welcome reprieve.

But what I loved most about South Portland was its history. Standing at **Bug Light Park**, you could almost hear the echoes of World War II, when South Portland's shipyards built hundreds of Liberty ships. The lighthouse itself, affectionately known as Bug Light, had its own mystique. Local legends spoke of it being haunted by the wife of a lighthouse keeper; her spirit said to linger along the shoreline.

South Portland also played a key role in the Underground Railroad. Willard Beach and the surrounding area were part of a network that helped enslaved people escape to freedom in Canada. Walking these same paths, I often felt a deep respect for the courage and humanity that shaped this chapter of Maine's history.

## WHERE STORIES COME TO LIFE

Portland's neighborhoods aren't just places—they're pieces of a larger story woven together by history, community, and a love of the small details that make life meaningful. From my home in the West End to the cobblestones of the Old Port, each neighborhood added something unique to my experience of living in this city. As we move forward, the next chapter will reveal how Portland transforms with the seasons, offering fresh experiences year-round. Get ready to see the city in a whole new light.

**3**

# SEASONAL HIGHLIGHTS

## A CITY FOR ALL SEASONS

Portland, Maine, isn't just a city that changes with the seasons—it embraces them fully, transforming into a new adventure every few months. In summer, the town comes alive with festivals, outdoor dining, and sun-soaked beach days. Fall turns Portland into a fiery masterpiece, with leaf-peeping, harvest celebrations, and cozy nights under crisp skies. Winter brings twinkling lights, holiday magic, and a festive buzz that rivals the snow-globe charm of a postcard. And spring? Spring is all about fresh beginnings, with blooming gardens, farmers markets, and the return of patio season. Whether you're strolling along cobblestone streets or kayaking in Casco Bay, every season in Portland has something spectacular to offer.

## SUMMER: SUN, SURF, AND CELEBRATION

Summer in Portland is all about endless days under the sun, outdoor festivals, and the salty tang of the ocean breeze. Whether you're exploring beaches, savoring fresh seafood, or dancing to live music at a festival, Portland knows how to make summer unforgettable.

- **Beaches and Islands:** Start your day at **Willard Beach** (Willard St, South Portland, ME), a family-friendly gem with calm waters perfect for wading. For an adventure, take the ferry to **Peaks Island** with **Casco Bay Lines** (56 Commercial St, Portland, ME | +1 207-774-7871). Rent bikes to explore its hidden beaches and visit the quirky **Umbrella Cover Museum** (62B Island Ave, Peaks Island, ME | +1 207-939-6518).
- **Festivals and Celebrations:** Portland's **Old Port Festival** is a summer tradition that turns the cobblestone streets into a carnival of food trucks, live music, and artisan booths. Held annually in June, it's the perfect way to kick off the season.
- **Harbor Cruises:** For a unique perspective of the city, hop on a sunset cruise with Casco Bay Lines. Watching the skyline shimmer in the golden light of dusk is an experience you won't forget.
- **Outdoor Dining:** Portland's culinary scene shines in summer. Grab a lobster roll from **Eventide Oyster Co.** (86 Middle St, Portland, ME | +1 207-774-8538) and enjoy it on their outdoor patio, or sample small plates at **Fore Street** (288 Fore St, Portland, ME | +1 207-775-2717) while soaking up the warm evening air.

## FALL: A SYMPHONY OF COLORS AND FESTIVITIES

Autumn in Portland is a feast for the senses, with brilliant foliage, harvest festivals, and crisp air that seems to carry the scent of apples and woodsmoke. It's a season that invites you to slow down, savor the beauty around you, and embrace the coziness of fall traditions.

- **Leaf-Peeping Adventures:** Within the city, **Baxter Boulevard** offers stunning views of Back Cove framed by vibrant trees. For a serene walk surrounded by autumn colors, visit **Mackworth Island** (Mackworth Island Trail, Falmouth, ME). A short drive away, **Wolfe's Neck Woods State Park**

(426 Wolfe's Neck Rd, Freeport, ME | +1 207-865-4465) provides trails that blend fall foliage with coastal views. Farther afield, drives through the **Golden Road** near Millinocket reveal panoramic vistas that are among the best in New England.

- **Apple Picking and Pumpkin Patches:** Fall weekends were made for visits to **Libby & Son U-Picks** (86 Sawyer Mountain Rd, Limerick, ME | +1 207-793-4749), where you can pick apples, enjoy fresh cider donuts, and take hayrides. Pumpkin patches like **Pineland Farms** (15 Farm View Dr, New Gloucester, ME | +1 207-688-4539) offer family-friendly activities like corn mazes and harvest festivals.
- **Seasonal Celebrations:** The **Cumberland County Fair** (197 Blanchard Rd, Cumberland, ME | +1 207-829-5531) is a highlight of the season, blending agricultural traditions with carnival fun.
- **Gardening Tours:** For green thumbs, the **Woodfords Community Garden Tour** offers a glimpse into over ten gardens in the Woodfords Corner area. Held annually in June, this self-guided tour showcases the creativity and dedication of local gardeners.

## WINTER: HOLIDAY MAGIC AND COZY RETREATS

When the snow falls, Portland transforms into a twinkling wonderland. Holiday lights illuminate historic streets, cozy cafés beckon with steaming drinks, and festivals celebrate the warmth of community amidst the chill of winter.

- **Holiday Lights and Festivities:** Downtown Portland shines with the **Winter City Lights** program, designed by local artist Pandora LaCasse. Walk through Congress Square and Monument Square to see the stunning light displays.
- **Victorian Mansion's Christmas Exhibit:** The **Victoria Mansion** (109 Danforth St, Portland, ME | +1 207-772-4841) becomes a holiday masterpiece every year, with each room

extravagantly decorated by local designers. It's a must-see for anyone who loves Christmas magic.

- **Christmas Boat Parade of Lights:** One of Portland's most festive events is the annual boat parade in Casco Bay. Watch from the Maine State Pier as brightly decorated boats sail by, spreading holiday cheer.
- **Day Trip to Strawbery Banke Museum:** Located in Portsmouth, NH, the **Strawbery Banke Museum** (14 Hancock St, Portsmouth, NH | +1 603-433-1100) is worth the trip for its stunningly decorated historic homes and outdoor skating rink.
- **Outdoor Adventures:** Winter fun in Portland includes sledding at **Payson Park** and ice skating at **Thompson's Point** (10 Thompson's Point Rd, Portland, ME | +1 207-747-5288). Afterward, warm up with a mulled cider from **The North Point** (35 Silver St, Portland, ME | +1 207-899-3778).

## SPRING: FRESH BEGINNINGS AND BLOOMING BEAUTY

Spring in Portland feels like a fresh start. The city shakes off the chill of winter, replacing snow with blooms and bare trees with lush greenery. It's a season that invites exploration and renewal.

- **Farmers Markets:** The **Portland Farmers Market** (Deering Oaks Park | +1 207-838-3746) is the beating heart of spring, filled with fresh produce, handmade goods, and vibrant flowers.
- **Gardens and Tours:** The **McLaughlin Garden & Homestead** (97 Main St, South Paris, ME | +1 207-743-8820) bursts into color with tulips, daffodils, and lilacs. Closer to home, the **Longfellow Garden** next to the Wadsworth-Longfellow House (489 Congress St, Portland, ME) offers a serene escape amidst the city.
- **Art in Bloom Festival:** Each spring, the **Portland Museum of Art** (7 Congress Square, Portland, ME | +1 207-775-6148) hosts this event, where floral designers create

arrangements inspired by the museum's artworks. It's a fragrant and visually stunning celebration of art and nature.
- **Outdoor Dining:** Spring marks the return of patio season in Portland. Grab a seat outside at **Fore Street** or **Central Provisions** (414 Fore St, Portland, ME | +1 207-805-1085) and enjoy a meal with the gentle warmth of the sun on your face.

## NIGHTLIFE (ANY SEASON OF THE YEAR): A BLEND OF TRADITION AND MODERNITY

Portland's nightlife is as dynamic as the city itself, with options ranging from lively music venues to intimate cocktail bars.

- **Live Music:** Venues like **One Longfellow Square** (181 State St, Portland, ME | +1 207-761-1757) and **State Theatre** (609 Congress St, Portland, ME | +1 207-956-6000) host performances ranging from local indie bands to international stars.
- **Bars and Breweries: Novare Res Bier Café** (4 Canal Plaza, Portland, ME | +1 207-761-2437) is a haven for craft beer lovers, while **The North Point** offers a cozy spot for handcrafted cocktails and small plates.

## A CITY IN EVERY SEASON

Portland is a city that celebrates every season with open arms. Whether you're basking in the golden glow of summer, marveling at the kaleidoscope of fall foliage, soaking up holiday magic in winter, or savoring the renewal of spring, there's always something to discover. As we move forward, this guide will explore the many ways to experience Portland, tailored to every kind of traveler. Get ready to plan your perfect adventure.

# PART 2: EXPERIENCES FOR EVERY TRAVELER

**4**

# WEEKEND WARRIORS

## PORTLAND IN 48 HOURS

**I**magine this: You've arrived in Portland with just a weekend to explore. The cobblestone streets of the Old Port stretch before you; the salty breeze carries the promise of fresh seafood, and the city hums with the energy of possibilities. Two days might not seem like much, but in Portland, every hour is packed with flavor, history, and adventure. With a carefully planned itinerary—and a bit of insider knowledge—you can soak up the best this city has to offer in just 48 hours.

## DAY 1: COASTAL CHARM AND CULINARY DELIGHTS

### Morning: Strolling the Old Port

Start your Portland adventure in the Old Port, the city's historic waterfront district. The cobblestone streets, lined with brick buildings, create a charming backdrop for a leisurely morning walk. Begin with coffee at **Bard Coffee** (185 Middle St, Portland, ME | +1 207-899-4788), where the aroma of freshly roasted beans is enough to wake you up. From there, wander into local shops like **Sherman's**

**Maine Coast Book Shop** (49 Exchange St, Portland, ME | +1 207-773-4100) for books and quirky souvenirs or **Lisa-Marie's Made in Maine** (35 Exchange St, Portland, ME | +1 207-828-1515) for locally crafted goods.

---

**Insider Tip:** Keep an eye out for the Old Port's underground history. It's rumored that tunnels once connected the waterfront to nearby buildings, used during Prohibition to smuggle alcohol. Some locals claim you can still spot hints of these secret passageways in the basements of certain shops.

---

## Midday: Food Tour Adventure

By now, your appetite has probably kicked in—perfect timing for a culinary exploration of Portland's food scene. Join a guided tour with **Maine Foodie Tours** (+1 207-233-7485), which offers tastings at iconic spots like **Eventide Oyster Co.** (86 Middle St, Portland, ME | +1 207-774-8538) for a mini lobster roll and **The Holy Donut** (7 Exchange St, Portland, ME | +1 207-775-7776) for a Maine potato donut.

---

**Fun Fact:** The Holy Donut's signature treat is made with real Maine potatoes, giving it a uniquely fluffy texture. Locals swear by the dark chocolate sea salt flavor.

---

## Afternoon: Portland Head Light and Cape Elizabeth

No trip to Portland is complete without visiting **Portland Head Light** (1000 Shore Rd, Cape Elizabeth, ME | +1 207-799-2661), Maine's most photographed lighthouse. Located in Fort Williams Park, just a 15-minute drive from downtown, it's the perfect spot for snapping iconic photos and taking in the coastal beauty. Explore the park's walking trails, enjoy a picnic, or grab a lobster roll from **Bite into Maine**, a popular food truck parked nearby.

**Personal Anecdote:** I'll never forget the time my daughter Channa, her husband Stephen, and I visited Portland Head Light during peak foliage season. The golden leaves framing the lighthouse made it feel like a scene straight out of a painting.

## Evening: Waterfront Dining

Return to the city for a waterfront dinner at **DiMillo's On the Water** (25 Long Wharf, Portland, ME | +1 207-772-2216), a floating restaurant housed in a converted ferry. Order the lobster bisque and enjoy the views of Casco Bay as the lights from the harbor sparkle on the water.

# DAY 2: ISLAND HOPPING AND SCENIC STROLLS

## Morning: Casco Bay Adventure

Start your second day with a ferry ride to **Peaks Island** with Casco Bay Lines (56 Commercial St, Portland, ME | +1 207-774-7871). Just 20 minutes from the mainland, Peaks Island offers a tranquil escape. Rent bikes from **Brad's Bike Rental** (+1 207-766-5631) and pedal along quiet roads to discover hidden beaches and sweeping ocean views.

**Ghost Story:** Locals whisper about a mysterious "Lady in White" said to roam Peaks Island, a remnant of its days as a summer retreat for Victorian vacationers. Some claim to have seen her near the island's old inns.

## Midday: Brunch with a View

After exploring, enjoy brunch at **The Cockeyed Gull** (78 Island Ave, Peaks Island, ME | +1 207-766-2800), a cozy spot with panoramic views of Casco Bay. Their crab cake Benedict is a crowd favorite.

## Afternoon: Eastern Promenade Stroll

Back in Portland, spend the afternoon on the **Eastern Promenade** (Eastern Promenade Trail, Portland, ME). This waterfront park offers stunning views of Casco Bay and a walking trail perfect for soaking up the coastal scenery. Stop by the **Portland Observatory** (138 Congress St, Portland, ME | +1 207-774-5561) for a glimpse into maritime history and breathtaking views from the top.

---

**Insider Tip:** The Eastern Promenade is a great spot for spotting seals in the bay—bring binoculars for a closer look!

---

## Evening: Breweries and Farewell Feast

End your weekend with a brewery crawl through Portland's celebrated craft beer scene. Start at **Allagash Brewing Company** (50 Industrial Way, Portland, ME | +1 207-878-5385) for a flight of Belgian-inspired beers, then head to **Bissell Brothers Brewing Company** (4 Thompsons Point, Portland, ME | +1 207-808-8258) for bold, hoppy IPAs.

For your farewell dinner, make a reservation at **Fore Street** (288 Fore St, Portland, ME | +1 207-775-2717). Their wood-fired dishes and seasonal menu are a perfect way to close out your weekend in Portland.

## TIPS FOR WEEKEND WARRIORS

- **Parking:** Street parking in Portland can be tricky, especially on weekends. Use the city's parking garages for a stress-free experience.
- **Reservations:** Portland's restaurants are popular—book ahead for prime spots like Fore Street or DiMillo's.
- **Packing Tip:** Comfortable walking shoes are a must for navigating Portland's cobblestones and island trails.

## MORE ADVENTURES AWAIT

A weekend in Portland offers a taste of everything this coastal city has to offer: history, flavors, and unforgettable views. As we move forward, this guide will dive deeper into experiences tailored to specific interests, from foodies to outdoor enthusiasts. Ready to find your perfect Portland adventure? Let's go.

**5**

# FOODIES AND CRAFT BEVERAGE ENTHUSIASTS

## PORTLAND'S FEAST FOR THE SENSES

For food lovers, Portland is the ultimate playground—a city where the culinary scene feels like an art form, and every bite tells a story. From buttery lobster rolls by the sea to world-class farm-to-table dining, Portland's reputation as a foodie haven is well-earned. And when you pair it with its thriving craft beverage scene—think award-winning breweries, inventive distilleries, and even urban wineries—it's easy to see why so many people leave the city with their taste buds forever changed.

## PORTLAND'S CULINARY ICONS: LOBSTER ROLLS, OYSTERS, AND CHOWDER

Portland's food scene has long been synonymous with its iconic seafood. Here are the must-try dishes—and where to find them:

- **Lobster Rolls:** Start with the classic. **Eventide Oyster Co.** (86 Middle St, Portland, ME | +1 207-774-8538) serves their signature brown butter lobster roll on a steamed bun—a decadent twist on the traditional version. If you prefer the classic split-top roll, head to **The Highroller Lobster Co.** (104 Exchange St, Portland, ME | +1 207-536-1623), where you can customize your roll with options like lime mayo or charred pineapple.

- **Clam Chowder:** A bowl of creamy clam chowder is practically a rite of passage. **Gilbert's Chowder House** (92 Commercial St, Portland, ME | +1 207-871-5636) is a local institution, serving hearty bowls brimming with fresh clams and just the right amount of bacon.
- **Oysters:** For a taste of Maine's freshest oysters, head to **The Shop—Raw Bar & Shellfish Market** (123 Washington Ave, Portland, ME | +1 207-536-7608), where you can slurp your way through a rotating selection of briny bivalves.

---

**Fun Fact:** Maine's cold waters produce some of the sweetest and plumpest oysters in the world. Each oyster farm has its own unique flavor profile based on its location—kind of like wine terroir, but for shellfish.

---

## FARM-TO-TABLE EXCELLENCE

Portland's chefs have embraced Maine's natural bounty, turning farm-to-table dining into a way of life. Here are a few of the best:

- **Fore Street:** (288 Fore St, Portland, ME | +1 207-775-2717) This James Beard Award-winning restaurant is a staple of Portland's dining scene. Their wood-fired dishes, crafted from locally sourced ingredients, showcase the best of Maine's farms and waters.
- **Central Provisions:** (414 Fore St, Portland, ME | +1 207-805-1085) Perfect for small plates and big flavors, this downtown spot features a creative menu that changes with the seasons.
- **Duckfat:** (43 Middle St, Portland, ME | +1 207-774-8080) Known for its legendary fries cooked in—you guessed it—

duck fat. Pair them with a local craft beer and one of their hearty paninis for the ultimate comfort meal.

- **Farmhouse Grill:** (40 Western Ave, Portland, ME | +1 207-555-3456) This hidden gem focuses on sustainably sourced meats and veggies, serving up dishes that are as wholesome as they are delicious.

## HIDDEN GEMS: FOOD TRUCKS, BAKERIES, AND DESSERT SPOTS

One of Portland's best-kept secrets is its vibrant food truck scene. During the warmer months, you'll find trucks parked around the city serving everything from gourmet tacos to handmade dumplings.

- **Tacos del Seoul:** This fusion food truck offers a creative mix of Korean and Mexican flavors, with dishes like bulgogi tacos and kimchi quesadillas.
- **Fishin' Ships:** Fried seafood gets a modern twist here, with dishes like haddock tacos and rosemary fries.

When it comes to bakeries, Portland knows how to do it right:

- **Standard Baking Co.:** (75 Commercial St, Portland, ME | +1 207-773-2112) Their almond croissants are legendary—flaky, buttery, and just the right amount of sweet.
- **Scratch Baking Co.:** (416 Preble St, South Portland, ME | +1 207-799-0668) A South Portland favorite known for its bagels, pastries, and inventive cookies.

If you're craving dessert:

- **The Holy Donut:** (7 Exchange St, Portland, ME | +1 207-775-7776) This beloved spot uses Maine potatoes to make their donuts uniquely fluffy.
- **Mount Desert Island Ice Cream:** (51 Exchange St, Portland, ME | +1 207-210-3432) Their inventive flavors, like

lemon curd ricotta or Maine sea salt caramel, are as memorable as they are delicious.

## THE CRAFT BEVERAGE SCENE: BREWERIES, DISTILLERIES, AND WINERIES

Portland's craft beverage scene is one of the best in the country, with options for every kind of drinker.

### Breweries

Portland is home to more breweries per capita than almost anywhere else in the U.S. Here are some must-visits:

- **Allagash Brewing Company:** (50 Industrial Way, Portland, ME | +1 207-878-5385) Known for its Belgian-inspired beers like the flagship Allagash White, this brewery is a staple of Portland's craft scene.
- **Bissell Brothers:** (4 Thompsons Point, Portland, ME | +1 207-808-8258) Fans of hoppy beers will love this spot, which specializes in juicy, aromatic IPAs.
- **Oxbow Blending & Bottling:** (49 Washington Ave, Portland, ME | +1 207-350-0025) For something a little different, head here for farmhouse ales and barrel-aged brews in a stylish industrial setting.

### Distilleries

If spirits are more your style, Portland has you covered:

- **Maine Craft Distilling:** (123 Washington Ave, Portland, ME | +1 207-899-0210) From blueberry moonshine to botanical gins, their inventive spirits capture the flavors of Maine.
- **Liquid Riot Bottling Company:** (250 Commercial St, Portland, ME | +1 207-221-8889) A brewery, distillery, and restaurant all in one. Try their house-made whiskey or rum while enjoying waterfront views.

### Urban Wineries

Wine enthusiasts won't be left out, thanks to Portland's urban wineries:

- **Cellardoor at the Point:** (4 Thompsons Point, Portland, ME | +1 207-536-7700) This elegant tasting room offers a wide selection of Maine-made wines, from dry reds to sweet dessert wines.

## PERSONAL TIPS AND FUN FACTS

- **Foodie Insider Tip:** Visit **Deering Oaks Park** on a Saturday morning for the **Portland Farmers Market**, where you can sample fresh cheeses, local honey, and handmade pastries.
- **Hidden Legend:** Some locals believe Portland's obsession with good food began with its seafaring roots. Fishermen returning from long voyages were said to throw elaborate feasts on the waterfront, using the best of their catch to celebrate their return.
- **Pro Tip for Beer Lovers:** Many breweries in Portland offer half-pours, so you can sample more of their offerings without overindulging.

## TASTING PORTLAND, ONE BITE AT A TIME

Portland isn't just a city—it's a flavor, a story told through its dishes and drinks. Whether you're indulging in a lobster roll by the harbor, sipping a craft beer at a bustling brewery, or enjoying a quiet moment with a croissant from a local bakery, the city's culinary scene leaves a lasting impression. In the next chapter, we'll explore the history behind some of Portland's most iconic landmarks, offering a glimpse into the past that shaped this vibrant city.

# 6

# HISTORY BUFFS

## HISTORY COMES ALIVE IN PORTLAND

Walking through Portland feels like stepping into a living museum, where every corner holds a story waiting to be uncovered. Whether it's the stately mansions of the West End, the bustling waterfront that once buzzed with trade, or the lighthouses that guided sailors home, Portland's history is woven into the fabric of the city. For history buffs, this is a place where the past feels alive, offering rich tales of resilience, maritime ingenuity, and cultural transformation.

## WALKING TOURS: STROLL THROUGH HISTORY

Portland's history is best explored on foot, and there's no shortage of walking tours to immerse you in the city's past.

- **Wadsworth-Longfellow House:** (489 Congress St, Portland, ME | +1 207-774-1822) Step into the childhood home of poet Henry Wadsworth Longfellow, a beautifully preserved 18th-century house filled with original furnishings and artifacts. Guided tours provide fascinating insights into Longfellow's life and the family's role in shaping Portland's cultural legacy.

- **Historic Old Port Tour:** Explore the cobblestone streets and learn about Portland's transformation from a bustling maritime hub to a modern-day foodie haven. Many tours delve into the city's lesser-known history, including its role in Prohibition and the underground tunnels rumored to connect the Old Port's buildings.

---

**Fun Fact:** The Great Fire of 1866, one of the worst urban fires in U.S. history, started in the Old Port. It destroyed much of the city but spurred Portland's remarkable rebuilding efforts, including the brick architecture that defines the district today.

---

## MARITIME HERITAGE: ANCHORS OF THE PAST

Portland's location on Casco Bay made it a vital hub for maritime trade and shipbuilding. Today, its seafaring legacy is preserved in museums and historic sites.

- **Maine Historical Society:** (489 Congress St, Portland, ME | +1 207-774-1822) Located adjacent to the Wadsworth-Longfellow House, this museum offers exhibits on Portland's history, from its Indigenous roots to its maritime and industrial growth. Don't miss the Brown Research Library, a treasure trove for history enthusiasts.
- **Maine Maritime Museum:** (243 Washington St, Bath, ME | +1 207-443-1316) About 40 minutes from Portland, this museum delves into Maine's shipbuilding history with interactive exhibits, historic boats, and even a full-size replica of a shipyard.

**Personal Anecdote:** Visiting the Maine Maritime Museum with my daughter Channa felt like traveling back in time. We were awestruck by the sheer scale of the shipyard exhibits and spent hours imagining what life was like for the sailors and builders who once called this industry home.

## PORTLAND OBSERVATORY: A TOWER OF HISTORY

Standing tall on Munjoy Hill, the **Portland Observatory** (138 Congress St, Portland, ME | +1 207-774-5561) is the last surviving maritime signal tower in the United States. Built in 1807, it played a crucial role in Portland's maritime economy, allowing signalmen to spot ships approaching the harbor and relay messages to the waterfront.

**Fun Fact:** The Observatory was never intended as a lighthouse—it's a signal tower, unique in its design and purpose. Climb to the top for panoramic views of the city and Casco Bay, and imagine what it must have been like to spot incoming ships after months at sea.

## VICTORIA MANSION: A GILDED AGE GEM

Also known as the Morse-Libby House, the **Victoria Mansion** (109 Danforth St, Portland, ME | +1 207-772-4841) is one of the finest examples of Italianate architecture in the United States. Built in the mid-19th century, this opulent mansion was a summer retreat for wealthy merchant Ruggles Sylvester Morse.

Each room is a masterpiece of craftsmanship, from the intricate woodwork to the hand-painted ceilings. During the holidays, the mansion becomes a wonderland of Victorian Christmas decorations, with each room transformed by local designers.

---

**Personal Tip:** Visit during the holiday season when the mansion is dressed to impress. It's a magical way to experience Portland's history and celebrate its festive spirit.

---

## LIGHTHOUSES AND FORTS: GUARDIANS OF THE COAST

Portland's lighthouses and historic forts tell the story of its strategic importance as a coastal city.

- **Portland Head Light:** (1000 Shore Rd, Cape Elizabeth, ME | +1 207-799-2661) Maine's oldest lighthouse, commissioned by George Washington, is a must-see. Located in Fort Williams Park, it offers stunning views of Casco Bay and a small museum housed in the former keeper's quarters.
- **Fort Gorges:** Accessible only by boat, this granite fort was built during the Civil War but never saw combat. Today, it stands as a hauntingly beautiful ruin, perfect for adventurous history buffs. Guided kayak tours are available through companies like **Portland Paddle** (East End Beach, Portland, ME | +1 207-370-9730).

---

**Ghost Story:** Fort Gorges is said to be haunted by the spirits of soldiers who were stationed there. Some visitors claim to hear whispers and footsteps echoing through the empty halls.

---

## HIDDEN GEMS: UNEARTHING THE UNEXPECTED

Portland is full of lesser-known historical sites that offer a deeper dive into the city's past:

- **Eastern Cemetery:** (224 Congress St, Portland, ME | +1 207-956-1457) One of Portland's oldest burial grounds, dating back to 1668. It's the final resting place for many of the city's early settlers and Revolutionary War soldiers. Ghost tours here are both chilling and fascinating.

- **Union Station Clock:** Though Union Station itself was demolished in 1961, its clock remains as a monument to Portland's golden age of train travel. You'll find it in Congress Square, a quiet reminder of a bygone era.

---

**Insider Tip:** Combine a visit to Eastern Cemetery with a stop at **Coffee by Design** (1 Diamond St, Portland, ME | +1 207-780-6767), a locally loved spot for grabbing a cup of joe before diving into the city's historic landmarks.

---

## TIPS FOR HISTORY BUFFS

- **Best Time to Visit:** Portland's historical sites are most accessible in late spring through early fall when the weather is mild, and attractions like the Portland Observatory and Victoria Mansion are open to the public.
- **Walking Shoes:** Many of Portland's historic landmarks are best explored on foot, so comfortable shoes are a must.
- **Guided Tours:** Consider joining a guided tour for deeper insights—local guides often share fascinating anecdotes and legends you won't find in guidebooks.

## A CITY SHAPED BY ITS PAST

Portland's history isn't confined to museums—it's written in its streets, its lighthouses, and its people. As you explore these landmarks, you'll gain a deeper appreciation for the events and individuals who shaped this remarkable city. In the next chapter, we'll shift gears to Portland's natural beauty, highlighting the outdoor adventures that await in this coastal paradise.

# 7

# OUTDOOR ENTHUSIASTS AND NATURE LOVERS

## NATURE AT YOUR DOORSTEP

Portland, Maine, isn't just a city on the coast—it's a gateway to some of New England's most breathtaking natural landscapes. From serene parks with waterfront views to adventurous hiking trails and tranquil lakes, Portland offers endless opportunities for outdoor enthusiasts. Whether you're paddling through the calm waters of Casco Bay, spotting rare birds in their natural habitats, or hiking up mountains with panoramic vistas, this city and its surroundings have something for every nature lover.

## PORTLAND'S BEST PARKS AND OUTDOOR SPACES

Portland's parks are perfect for unwinding, getting active, or simply soaking up the scenery.

- **Eastern Promenade:** (Eastern Promenade Trail, Portland, ME) This waterfront gem on Munjoy Hill offers stunning views of Casco Bay, making it a favorite for locals and visitors alike. The paved trail is ideal for walking, running, or biking, and the grassy lawns are perfect for picnics. Don't miss Fort Allen Park within the promenade, a historic spot with cannons and sweeping ocean views.

- **Back Cove Trail:** This flat, 3.5-mile loop encircles Back Cove and offers stunning views of Portland's skyline. It's a peaceful spot for a morning jog or a leisurely stroll, with benches along the way to pause and enjoy the scenery.

---

**Insider Tip:** Visit Back Cove Trail at sunrise for a spectacular view of the city bathed in golden light—an experience that feels almost magical.

---

- **Deering Oaks Park:** (Park Ave, Portland, ME) A historic park in the heart of the city, Deering Oaks features walking paths, duck ponds, and even a seasonal farmers market. It's a favorite for families, with plenty of green space to spread out and relax.

## WATER ACTIVITIES: KAYAKING, PADDLEBOARDING, AND WHALE WATCHING

Portland's coastal location makes it a paradise for water lovers.

- **Kayaking and Paddleboarding:** Rent gear from **Portland Paddle** (East End Beach, Portland, ME | +1 207-370-9730) and explore the calm waters of Casco Bay. Paddle around islands, discover hidden coves and even spot seals lounging on rocky outcroppings.

---

**Personal Anecdote:** On one paddling adventure, my daughter Channa and I came across a pod of porpoises just off Peaks Island. Watching them playfully leap through the water felt like a moment straight out of a nature documentary.

---

- **Whale Watching:** Book a tour with **Odyssey Whale Watch** (170 Commercial St, Portland, ME | +1 207-775-0727) to see humpback whales, fin whales, and dolphins in their natural habitat. These tours often include fascinating insights from marine biologists about the ecosystem of the Gulf of Maine.

---

**Fun Fact:** The Gulf of Maine is one of the most productive marine ecosystems in the world, making it a prime spot for whale watching during the summer months.

---

## DAY TRIPS: SEBAGO LAKE AND THE WHITE MOUNTAINS

Portland's proximity to incredible natural wonders makes it an ideal base for day trips.

- **Sebago Lake State Park:** (11 Park Access Rd, Casco, ME | +1 207-693-6231) Just 40 minutes from Portland, Sebago Lake is a haven for water activities like swimming, boating, and fishing. With sandy beaches and clear waters, it's a perfect spot for families or anyone looking to relax by the water.
- **White Mountains Hiking Trails:** About an hour and a half from Portland, the White Mountains in New Hampshire offer hiking trails for all skill levels. **Mount Willard Trail** in Crawford Notch is a relatively easy hike with stunning views, while the more challenging **Franconia Ridge Loop** provides jaw-dropping vistas that make every step worth it.

---

**Insider Tip:** Pack a picnic for your hike, featuring treats from the Portland Farmers Market or a local bakery like **Standard Baking Co.** (75 Commercial St, Portland, ME | +1 207-773-2112).

---

## BIRDWATCHING AND PRESERVED NATURAL HABITATS

For those who love wildlife, Portland is a birdwatcher's paradise.

- **Capisic Pond Park:** (Capisic St, Portland, ME) This peaceful park is a hidden gem for spotting migratory birds and other wildlife. Bring binoculars and watch for species like herons, egrets, and warblers.
- **Gilsland Farm Audubon Center:** (20 Gilsland Farm Rd, Falmouth, ME | +1 207-781-2330) Just a 10-minute drive from downtown Portland, this 65-acre nature preserve features walking trails, meadows, and salt marshes. It's a prime spot for birdwatching, especially during migration seasons.

---

**Fun Fact:** Maine is home to over 300 bird species, making it one of the top states for birdwatching in the U.S.

---

- **Rachel Carson National Wildlife Refuge:** (321 Port Rd, Wells, ME | +1 207-646-9226) About 45 minutes from Portland, this refuge honors the legacy of environmentalist Rachel Carson. Its salt marshes and estuaries are teeming with wildlife, offering peaceful trails for nature lovers.

## HIDDEN GEMS FOR OUTDOOR ENTHUSIASTS

- **Jewell Island:** Accessible by kayak or small boat, Jewell Island in Casco Bay offers hiking trails, secluded beaches, and historic World War II observation towers. It's a peaceful retreat for adventurous explorers.
- **Mackworth Island:** (Falmouth, ME) This tiny island, connected to the mainland by a causeway, features an easy walking trail with stunning ocean views. It's also home to a "Fairy House Village," where visitors are encouraged to build their own whimsical creations.

**Personal Anecdote:** My daughter and I spent an afternoon on Mackworth Island building fairy houses from driftwood and seashells. It was a simple but magical way to connect with nature —and each other.

## SEASONAL OUTDOOR ACTIVITIES

No matter the time of year, Portland offers outdoor adventures:

- **Winter:** Try snowshoeing at **Pineland Farms** (15 Farm View Dr, New Gloucester, ME | +1 207-688-4539), where groomed trails wind through picturesque forests and fields.
- **Spring:** Explore the blooming gardens at **McLaughlin Garden & Homestead** (97 Main St, South Paris, ME | +1 207-743-8820), or take a hike through Wolfe's Neck Woods to see the first signs of new life.
- **Summer:** Kayaking, paddleboarding, and harbor cruises take center stage.
- **Fall:** Leaf-peeping hikes in the White Mountains or a serene paddle through Casco Bay's foliage-framed waters make this season unforgettable.

## TIPS FOR OUTDOOR ENTHUSIASTS

- **Pack Smart:** Bring sunscreen, bug spray, and plenty of water for summer activities. In colder months, layers are key.
- **Respect Wildlife:** Observe animals from a distance and avoid feeding them to ensure their safety and yours.
- **Early Starts:** Popular trails and parks can get crowded— arrive early to enjoy the serenity of nature.

## NATURE AND BEYOND

Portland's outdoor offerings go beyond recreation—they're an invitation to reconnect with the natural world. From serene parks to thrilling adventures, the city and its surroundings have something for everyone. In the next chapter, we'll explore Portland's artistic soul, delving into its galleries, performances, and cultural events that make it a hub for creative expression.

# 8

# ART AND CULTURE AFICIONADOS

## PORTLAND'S CREATIVE SOUL

Art and culture flow through Portland like the tide, ever-present and ever-changing. From historic theaters and bustling art walks to internationally recognized museums and captivating murals, the city is a hub for creativity. Whether you're a seasoned connoisseur or someone who simply loves being surrounded by beauty and innovation, Portland has something to offer at every turn.

## ART GALLERIES, MURALS, AND INSTALLATIONS

Portland's streets and galleries tell stories through color, form, and expression.

- **Congress Street Murals:** A stroll along Congress Street reveals vibrant murals that turn the city into an open-air gallery. One standout is the colorful "Piece by Piece" mural, a collaboration by artists Greta Bank and Pat Corrigan, which celebrates Portland's diversity and creativity.

- **SPACE Gallery:** (538 Congress St, Portland, ME | +1 207-828-5600) Known for its edgy and experimental vibe, SPACE Gallery is a must-visit for fans of contemporary art. Their rotating exhibits, live performances, and film screenings push creative boundaries.
- **Ocean Gateway Murals:** The Ocean Gateway area features large-scale murals inspired by Portland's maritime history. The pieces, created by local and international artists, add a splash of vibrancy to the waterfront.

---

**Insider Tip:** Many murals are hidden in alleys or side streets, so be sure to explore off the beaten path—you might stumble upon a hidden masterpiece.

---

## THE PORTLAND MUSEUM OF ART: A CULTURAL CROWN JEWEL

At the heart of Portland's art scene is the **Portland Museum of Art** (7 Congress Square, Portland, ME | +1 207-775-6148). With a collection spanning over 18,000 works, the museum showcases pieces from American and European masters, as well as modern and contemporary artists.

**Must-See Highlights:**

- Works by Winslow Homer, a Maine native whose paintings capture the rugged beauty of the state's coast.
- Edgar Degas' "Dancer Adjusting Her Shoe" a serene yet dynamic portrayal of a ballet dancer.
- The museum's rotating exhibits which have included everything from impressionist landscapes to avant-garde installations.

---

**Fun Fact:** The museum owns and operates the Winslow Homer

Studio in Prouts Neck, where visitors can see where the artist lived and worked.

**Personal Tip:** Visit on Free Fridays (from 4 p.m. to 8 p.m.) to enjoy the museum without an entry fee. It's a great way to soak up culture on a budget.

## PERFORMING ARTS: THEATER, MUSIC, AND MORE

Portland's performing arts scene is as lively as its visual art offerings, with something for every taste.

- **Merrill Auditorium:** (20 Myrtle St, Portland, ME | +1 207-842-0800) This grand venue hosts the **Portland Symphony Orchestra**, whose performances range from classical masterpieces to themed pops concerts. Holiday favorites like the **Magic of Christmas** are a beloved local tradition.
- **Portland Stage:** (25A Forest Ave, Portland, ME | +1 207-774-0465) Maine's largest professional theater company offers an eclectic mix of classic plays, contemporary works, and original productions.
- **State Theatre:** (609 Congress St, Portland, ME | +1 207-956-6000) This historic venue is a hotspot for live music, featuring acts from indie bands to big name artists.

**Personal Anecdote:** I remember attending a performance of "Our Town" at Portland Stage with my daughter Channa. The intimate setting and powerful acting left us both moved—it was one of those rare nights where the theater felt like pure magic.

## CULTURAL FESTIVALS: CELEBRATING CREATIVITY

Portland's festivals bring its artistic energy to life, offering immersive experiences for locals and visitors alike.

- **First Friday Art Walk:** Held on the first Friday of each month, this citywide event invites galleries, studios, and museums to open their doors for free. The streets buzz with live music, pop-up art exhibits, and food vendors, creating a festive atmosphere.
- **Maine International Film Festival:** (Waterville, ME | +1 207-861-8138) A short drive from Portland, this annual event showcases the best in independent and international cinema. It's a must for film enthusiasts, with Q&A sessions, workshops, and special appearances by filmmakers.
- **Portland Fine Craft Show:** This outdoor festival on Congress Street highlights the work of talented artisans, from jewelers and ceramicists to textile artists. It's a wonderful opportunity to meet makers and purchase one-of-a-kind pieces.
- **Harvest on the Harbor:** Celebrating Maine's food and drink culture, this October festival also features local artists and musicians. It's a unique blend of culinary and cultural creativity.

---

**Insider Tip:** Arrive early for First Friday Art Walk to secure parking and beat the crowds at popular galleries.

---

## Hidden Gems for Art Lovers

- **Cryptozoology Museum:** (4 Thompsons Point, Portland, ME | +1 207-518-9496) This quirky museum explores the art and folklore of mythical creatures like Bigfoot and the Loch Ness Monster. It's a playful, offbeat addition to Portland's cultural scene.
- **The Maine Jewish Museum:** (267 Congress St, Portland, ME | +1 207-773-2339) This small but impactful museum highlights the stories of Maine's Jewish community through art and historical exhibits.

- **Street Art Tours:** Local guides offer walking tours focused on Portland's street art, sharing the stories behind the murals and the artists who created them.

---

**Personal Anecdote:** One of my favorite discoveries was a tiny mosaic of a lobster hidden on a brick wall near Commercial Street. It felt like finding a secret treasure in the middle of the city.

---

## Tips for Art and Culture Enthusiasts

- **Check Local Listings:** Many performances and exhibits are seasonal, so keep an eye on local calendars like **Portland Old Port** or **Visit Portland** for the latest updates.
- **Engage with Artists:** Many galleries and events encourage interaction with artists—don't be shy about asking questions or sharing your thoughts on their work.
- **Explore Beyond Downtown:** Neighborhoods like East Bayside and the West End often have pop-up galleries and smaller art spaces worth checking out.

## A CREATIVE JOURNEY AWAITS

Portland's art and culture scene is a celebration of creativity in all its forms. From world-class museums to hidden murals intimate theater productions to bustling festivals, every experience feels like a window into the city's soul. As we move forward, we'll shift our focus to families, exploring kid-friendly adventures and attractions that prove Portland is a destination for all ages.

# FAMILIES

## A CITY FOR ALL AGES

Portland, Maine, is the kind of city where families can find fun and adventure around every corner. Whether you're exploring hands-on museums, building sandcastles at the beach, or learning about the city's storied past through interactive experiences, Portland strikes the perfect balance of education and entertainment for visitors of all ages. With its cozy restaurants, safe streets, and welcoming vibe, it's a destination that makes traveling with kids a breeze.

## KID-FRIENDLY ATTRACTIONS

Portland offers a variety of attractions designed to engage, educate, and entertain children:

- **Children's Museum & Theatre of Maine:** (250 Thompson's Point Rd, Portland, ME | +1 207-828-1234) This vibrant space at Thompson's Point combines a children's museum and a theater into one interactive experience. Kids can explore hands-on exhibits about science, art, and the environment, then catch a family-friendly production in the on-site theater.

---

**Insider Tip:** Check the schedule for workshops and activities, like the popular "Messy Art Studio," which lets kids unleash their creativity.

---

- **Portland Science Center:** (68 Commercial St, Portland, ME | +1 207-812-3866) Located on the waterfront, the Science Center offers rotating exhibits that cover everything from dinosaurs to space exploration. It's a great spot for curious minds who love to learn through interactive displays.
- **Portland Public Library:** (5 Monument Square, Portland, ME | +1 207-871-1700) The children's section of the library is a hidden gem, offering storytime events, crafts, and activities for younger visitors.

---

**Fun Fact:** The Portland Public Library is one of the oldest public libraries in the U.S., dating back to 1867.

---

## OUTDOOR ACTIVITIES FOR FAMILIES

Portland's parks, beaches, and trails are perfect for families who love to explore the outdoors.

- **Deering Oaks Park:** (Park Ave, Portland, ME) This historic park has everything from playgrounds to duck ponds, making it a favorite for families. During the summer, kids can cool off in the splash pad while parents enjoy the shade of the park's towering oak trees.

- **Willard Beach:** (South Portland, ME) Just a short drive from downtown, this sandy beach is ideal for young children thanks to its calm waters and tidal pools. Bring a bucket and shovel for hours of seaside fun.
- **Eastern Promenade:** (Eastern Promenade Trail, Portland, ME) Families can enjoy picnics, bike rides, and breathtaking views of Casco Bay. The nearby playground is a great spot for younger kids to burn off some energy.
- **Nature Walks:** For a peaceful escape, head to **Mackworth Island** (Falmouth, ME), where the easy trail is perfect for little legs. Kids will love spotting birds and building fairy houses along the way.

---

**Personal Anecdote:** One of my favorite memories is walking the Eastern Promenade trail with my daughter Channa right after my granddaughter Vera was born. We stopped to watch sailboats in the bay, it was such lovely weather as we watched the sailboats and yachts and talked about how life was about to change for her and Stephen.

---

## EDUCATIONAL EXPERIENCES

Portland offers plenty of opportunities for learning disguised as fun:

- **Portland Head Light:** (1000 Shore Rd, Cape Elizabeth, ME | +1 207-799-2661) Maine's most iconic lighthouse is a must-visit for families. Kids will enjoy exploring the nearby trails and looking out over the rugged coastline, while adults can dive into the rich maritime history at the on-site museum.
- **Eco-Tours:** Join an eco-tour with **Portland Paddle** (East End Beach, Portland, ME | +1 207-370-9730) or **Lucky Catch Cruises** (170 Commercial St, Portland, ME | +1 207-761-0941). These hands-on experiences teach kids about Maine's marine life, from lobsters to seals.

- **Historic Sites:** Explore the **Wadsworth-Longfellow House** (489 Congress St, Portland, ME | +1 207-774-1822) for a glimpse into 18th-century life or take a ferry to **Fort Gorges**, where kids can pretend to be explorers as they wander through the ruins of this Civil War-era fort.

---

**Fun Fact:** Portland Head Light was commissioned by George Washington in 1791, making it one of the oldest lighthouses in the U.S.

---

## FAMILY-FRIENDLY DINING

Portland's dining scene caters to all ages, with plenty of spots that offer kids' menus and welcoming atmospheres.

- **Flatbread Company:** (72 Commercial St, Portland, ME | +1 207-772-8777) Located on the waterfront, this pizza spot is a hit with families. Kids can watch the wood-fired ovens in action while enjoying delicious organic flatbreads.
- **Becky's Diner:** (390 Commercial St, Portland, ME | +1 207-773-7070) A Portland institution, this casual diner serves hearty breakfasts and classic comfort food in a relaxed setting.
- **Duckfat:** (43 Middle St, Portland, ME | +1 207-774-8080) Known for its incredible fries and milkshakes, Duckfat is a hit with both kids and parents.
- **Gelato Fiasco:** (425 Fore St, Portland, ME | +1 207-699-4314) End your meal with a sweet treat from this beloved gelato shop, which offers a variety of creative flavors.

---

**Insider Tip:** Many Portland restaurants are accommodating to families—don't hesitate to ask for kid-sized portions or special modifications.

---

## HIDDEN GEMS FOR FAMILIES

- **Bug Light Park:** (South Portland, ME) This park is home to the Portland Breakwater Lighthouse (affectionately called Bug Light) and offers open spaces for kite flying, picnicking, and stunning views of the harbor.
- **Thompson's Point:** This family-friendly hub features outdoor events, food trucks, and even an ice-skating rink in the winter. During the summer, it's a great spot to catch live music or enjoy the Sunday farmers market.
- **Children's Garden at Fort Williams Park:** (Cape Elizabeth, ME) A whimsical garden designed for kids, complete with natural play structures and a fairy house building area.

---

**Insider Tip:** Kids love Bug Light Park, especially running through the wide-open fields while watching ships pass in the harbor. It's one of those simple but unforgettable moments that make Portland so special for families.

---

## TIPS FOR FAMILY TRAVEL IN PORTLAND

- **Pack for All Weather:** Maine's weather can change quickly, so bring layers and rain gear to stay comfortable during outdoor activities.
- **Plan Ahead:** Many kid-friendly attractions, like the Children's Museum, require tickets or reservations, especially during busy seasons.
- **Relaxed Schedules:** Portland is a laid-back city, so embrace a flexible itinerary that allows time for unplanned discoveries.

## FUN FOR EVERYONE

Portland is a city that invites families to slow down, connect, and make memories together. From playful afternoons at the park to eye-opening eco-tours on the bay, there's no shortage of things to see and do for visitors of all ages. Next, we'll explore how Portland's charm extends to those traveling solo, with tips and ideas for discovering the city on your own.

$$10$$

# SOLO TRAVELERS

## DISCOVERING PORTLAND, ONE MOMENT AT A TIME

Traveling solo in Portland feels like an invitation to explore at your own pace. This is a city that lets you wander its cobblestone streets, linger over coffee in cozy cafés, and lose yourself in a good book at one of its charming bookstores. Whether you're seeking quiet solitude or hoping to meet like-minded adventurers on a group tour, Portland offers countless ways to make the most of your solo trip.

## COZY COFFEE SHOPS AND WI-FI-FRIENDLY SPACES

Solo travelers will feel right at home in Portland's many welcoming coffee shops, perfect for catching up on work, journaling your travel adventures, or simply savoring a quiet moment.

- **Tandem Coffee Roasters:** (742 Congress St, Portland, ME | +1 207-805-1887) Housed in a converted gas station, Tandem Coffee is as charming as it is delicious. Grab a latte and a homemade biscuit, and settle in at one of their sunny outdoor tables.

- **Bard Coffee:** (185 Middle St, Portland, ME | +1 207-899-4788) A favorite among locals and visitors alike, Bard Coffee offers strong brews and plenty of seating—ideal for working or people-watching.
- **Coffee By Design:** (1 Diamond St, Portland, ME | +1 207-780-6767) This Portland staple combines industrial charm with a quiet, productive vibe. It's the perfect spot for a laid-back afternoon with a book or laptop.

---

**Insider Tip:** Many of Portland's coffee shops roast their own beans, so don't forget to grab a bag to bring a taste of your trip back home.

---

## SOCIAL GROUP TOURS

Exploring Portland solo doesn't mean you have to go it alone. Group tours are a fantastic way to dive into the city's culture and connect with fellow travelers.

- **Maine Foodie Tours:** (+1 207-233-7485) From walking food tours of the Old Port to specialty excursions like the "Boozy Brunch Tour," Maine Foodie Tours offers something for every palate.
- **Brewery Tours with The Maine Brew Bus:** (79 Commercial St, Portland, ME | +1 207-200-9111) This lively tour takes you behind the scenes of Portland's craft beer scene, with stops at multiple breweries and plenty of opportunities to mingle with other beer enthusiasts.
- **Portland's Hidden History Walking Tour:** This tour dives into the city's lesser-known stories, from underground tunnels to maritime legends. It's a great way to learn about Portland's past while meeting fellow history buffs.

**Personal Anecdote:** When I first moved to Portland, I joined a Maine Foodie Tour and ended up making friends from three different states. By the end of the evening, we were swapping travel stories over drinks and planning a group dinner for the next day.

## BOOKSTORES, THRIFT SHOPS, AND QUIET PARKS FOR SOLO EXPLORING

Portland is a haven for solo adventurers who love to wander. Its mix of independent shops, scenic parks, and tucked-away treasures make it an endlessly rewarding city to explore.

### Bookstores

- **Sherman's Maine Coast Book Shop:** (49 Exchange St, Portland, ME | +1 207-773-4100) Maine's oldest bookstore offers a cozy atmosphere and a well-curated selection of local literature, travel guides, and quirky gifts.
- **Longfellow Books:** (1 Monument Way, Portland, ME | +1 207-772-4045) Located near Monument Square, this independent bookstore is a favorite for its mix of new and used books.
- **Print: A Bookstore:** (273 Congress St, Portland, ME | +1 207-536-4778) A modern space with a strong focus on local authors and thoughtful recommendations from staff.

## THRIFT SHOPS AND UNIQUE FINDS

- **Material Objects:** (500 Congress St, Portland, ME | +1 207-775-1735) A treasure trove of vintage clothing, books, and home goods—perfect for a leisurely solo browse.
- **Portland Flea-for-All:** (585 Congress St, Portland, ME | +1 207-370-7570) This multi-vendor marketplace is a solo

shopper's dream, offering everything from antiques to handmade crafts.

---

**Fun Fact:** Portland's thriving thrift scene is partly fueled by its creative residents, who often repurpose and upcycle their finds into art.

---

## Quiet Parks for Reflection

- **Eastern Promenade:** (Eastern Promenade Trail, Portland, ME) Find a bench overlooking Casco Bay and let the sound of the waves clear your mind.
- **Capisic Pond Park:** (Capisic St, Portland, ME) This serene park is a hidden gem for nature lovers, offering peaceful trails and excellent birdwatching opportunities.
- **Western Promenade:** Located in the West End, this quiet park offers sweeping views of the Fore River and a peaceful escape from the city's hustle and bustle.

---

**Personal Anecdote:** On a sunny afternoon in the Western Promenade, I found myself sitting on a bench, chatting with a local artist who was sketching the view. We ended up trading travel tips, and I left with a new perspective on the city.

---

## HIDDEN GEMS FOR SOLO TRAVELERS

- **Portland Observatory:** (138 Congress St, Portland, ME | +1 207-774-5561) The climb to the top is worth it for the breathtaking views, and you'll often find other solo travelers eager to strike up a conversation.
- **Cryptozoology Museum:** (4 Thompsons Point, Portland, ME | +1 207-518-9496) This quirky museum is perfect for a solo

outing—its exhibits on mythical creatures are as fascinating as
they are fun.

- **Bug Light Park:** (South Portland, ME) A great spot for solo
reflection, this park offers scenic views of the harbor and the
adorable Portland Breakwater Lighthouse, affectionately
known as Bug Light.

## TIPS FOR SOLO TRAVELERS

- **Be Spontaneous:** Portland's size makes it easy to explore
without a strict plan—embrace the joy of wandering and see
where the city takes you.
- **Join a Meetup:** Check local listings for events like yoga
classes, art workshops, or trivia nights. It's a great way to meet
locals and other travelers.
- **Stay Central:** Choose accommodations near the Old Port or
Congress Street for easy access to the city's main attractions.

## EXPLORING ON YOUR OWN TERMS

Solo travel in Portland is a rewarding experience, offering a mix of
independence, discovery, and connection. From quiet moments in a
cozy coffee shop to lively group tours that introduce you to new
friends, the city welcomes solo adventurers with open arms. As we
move forward, we'll explore how Portland sets the stage for romance,
making it an ideal destination for couples seeking a memorable
getaway.

# 11

# ROMANTIC GETAWAY SEEKERS

## A CITY MADE FOR TWO

Portland, Maine, exudes a quiet, romantic charm that makes it the perfect destination for couples. From intimate dinners overlooking the water to cozy strolls along cobblestone streets, every corner of this coastal city seems designed for connection. Whether you're planning a honeymoon, celebrating an anniversary, or simply seeking time away together, Portland offers countless ways to make your getaway unforgettable.

## SCENIC DINING SPOTS FOR COUPLES

Portland's culinary scene is as romantic as it is delicious, with cozy bistros, waterfront views, and candlelit tables perfect for two.

- **Fore Street:** (288 Fore St, Portland, ME | +1 207-775-2717) This James Beard Award-winning restaurant is the epitome of rustic elegance. Their open kitchen, wood-fired dishes, and intimate atmosphere create a dining experience that's equal parts warm and luxurious.

- **DiMillo's on the Water:** (25 Long Wharf, Portland, ME | +1 207-772-2216) Set aboard a converted ferry, DiMillo's combines nautical charm with stunning views of Casco Bay. For a truly romantic touch, request a table by the window as the sun sets over the harbor.
- **Street & Co.:** (33 Wharf St, Portland, ME | +1 207-775-0887) Tucked away on a cobblestone alley, this Mediterranean-inspired seafood restaurant is known for its cozy ambiance and exquisite dishes, like lobster over linguine.
- **Scales:** (68 Commercial St, Portland, ME | +1 207-805-0444) For couples seeking waterfront elegance, Scales offers refined seafood in a stunning industrial-chic setting.

---

**Insider Tip:** Book your table early, especially at Fore Street or Street & Co., to secure a spot at these sought-after romantic restaurants.

---

## PRIVATE SUNSET CRUISES OR SAILBOAT CHARTERS

Nothing says romance quite like a sunset cruise or a private sail through Casco Bay.

- **Casco Bay Custom Charters:** (+1 207-205-5796) Book a private sailboat for just the two of you, complete with champagne and hors d'oeuvres as you glide past lighthouses and secluded islands.
- **Lucky Catch Cruises:** (170 Commercial St, Portland, ME | +1 207-761-0941) For a more interactive experience, join a lobster boat tour and help haul traps together—a uniquely Maine way to bond.
- **Portland Schooner Co.:** (56 Commercial St, Portland, ME | +1 207-766-2500) Step aboard a vintage schooner for a romantic evening sail. The gentle sway of the boat and the

sound of the waves create a serene backdrop for reconnecting with your partner.

---

**Personal Anecdote:** My good friends once chartered a sailboat through Casco Bay Custom Charters for their anniversary. Watching the sun dip below the horizon as they toasted with champagne was one of their favorite Portland memories.

---

## COUPLES-FRIENDLY WELLNESS SPAS AND BOUTIQUE ACCOMMODATIONS

Portland's spas and boutique hotels are designed with relaxation and romance in mind.

### Wellness Spas

- **Soakology:** (511 Congress St, Portland, ME | +1 207-879-7625) Treat yourselves to a foot soak and massage in a private room. The dim lighting and serene atmosphere make this spa a favorite for couples seeking quiet relaxation.
- **Nine Stones Spa:** (185 Fore St, Portland, ME | +1 207-772-8480) Indulge in a couples massage at this luxury spa, known for its tranquil setting and personalized treatments.

### Boutique Accommodations

- **The Press Hotel:** (119 Exchange St, Portland, ME | +1 207-808-8800) Housed in a former newspaper building, this boutique hotel combines chic design with nods to Portland's literary history. The cozy lounge area and on-site restaurant, UNION, add to the romantic vibe.
- **Portland Harbor Hotel:** (468 Fore St, Portland, ME | +1 207-775-9090) This upscale hotel offers elegantly designed rooms and a central location perfect for exploring the city hand-in-hand.

- **Blind Tiger:** (163 Danforth St, Portland, ME | +1 207-536-0415) For a more intimate stay, this boutique inn offers individually designed rooms in a historic mansion.

---

**Insider Tip:** Many boutique hotels in Portland offer romance packages that include extras like champagne, chocolate-covered strawberries, and late checkouts.

---

## SCENIC SPOTS FOR PROPOSALS AND INTIMATE PICNICS

Portland is filled with picturesque locations that feel straight out of a romance novel.

- **Portland Head Light:** (1000 Shore Rd, Cape Elizabeth, ME | +1 207-799-2661) As Maine's most iconic lighthouse, this spot is perfect for a proposal or a dreamy picnic. Bring a blanket and set up on the cliffs for stunning views of the ocean.
- **Eastern Promenade:** With its rolling green lawns and panoramic views of Casco Bay, the Eastern Promenade is a lovely setting for a quiet picnic. Pack treats from the **Portland Farmers Market** or grab sandwiches from **Rose Foods** (428 Forest Ave, Portland, ME | +1 207-835-0991).
- **Mackworth Island:** (Falmouth, ME) Take a leisurely stroll along the island's loop trail, then settle on the shore for a private picnic. The tranquil setting and ocean views make it a romantic escape just minutes from the city.
- **Bug Light Park:** (South Portland, ME) This park offers charming harbor views and a picturesque lighthouse, making it an ideal spot for popping the question or sharing a quiet moment together.

## HIDDEN GEMS FOR COUPLES

- **Battery Steele:** Located on Peaks Island, this historic fort is a unique and secluded spot to explore together. Bring a flashlight to wander through its graffiti-covered tunnels, then head to a nearby beach to watch the sunset.
- **Tandem Coffee + Bakery:** (742 Congress St, Portland, ME | +1 207-805-1887) This cozy café is perfect for a relaxed morning date. Share a biscuit and enjoy the charming atmosphere of this former gas station-turned-bakery.
- **Victoria Mansion:** (109 Danforth St, Portland, ME | +1 207-772-4841) Touring this opulent 19th-century home feels like stepping into another era. During the holidays, its elaborate decorations add an extra layer of romance.

### Tips for Romantic Travelers

- **Plan Ahead:** Popular restaurants and activities, like sunset cruises, book up quickly—reserve your spots early.
- **Pack a Blanket:** Many of Portland's most romantic spots are perfect for picnics or watching the stars.
- **Capture the Moment:** Consider hiring a local photographer for a couple's photo session at a scenic location like Portland Head Light.

## LOVE IN EVERY DETAIL

Portland's intimate charm and breathtaking scenery make it a city tailor-made for romance. Whether you're savoring a candlelit dinner, sailing under a starry sky, or sharing quiet moments by the sea, Portland creates the perfect backdrop for unforgettable memories. As we move forward, we'll explore how to enjoy this incredible city on a budget without sacrificing any of its magic.

**12**

# BUDGET-CONSCIOUS TRAVELERS

## PORTLAND ON A DIME

Traveling doesn't have to break the bank—especially in Portland, Maine. This city offers a treasure trove of experiences that won't drain your wallet, from free coastal views and vibrant parks to affordable dining that doesn't skimp on flavor. With some savvy planning and insider tips, you can enjoy the best of Portland while keeping your budget intact.

## FREE OR LOW-COST ATTRACTIONS

Portland is full of places to explore that won't cost you a penny—or very little.

- **Fort Allen Park and Eastern Promenade:** (Eastern Promenade Trail, Portland, ME) Overlooking Casco Bay, Fort Allen Park offers expansive views of the water and nearby islands. Bring a blanket and a picnic for a relaxing afternoon.
- **Willard Beach:** (South Portland, ME) This charming beach is a quiet escape where you can enjoy the sand and surf

without any fees. The tidal pools are perfect for families with kids or anyone who enjoys hunting for small marine life.

- **Mackworth Island:** (Falmouth, ME) A short drive from downtown, this island features a scenic loop trail that's perfect for walking and birdwatching. Entrance is just a small parking fee, making it a budget-friendly nature escape.
- **First Friday Art Walk:** Held on the first Friday of each month, this free event turns downtown into a celebration of art, with galleries, pop-up exhibits, and live performances.
- **Eastern Cemetery:** (224 Congress St, Portland, ME) Take a self-guided tour of this historic cemetery, where Revolutionary War soldiers and other notable figures are buried. It's a fascinating glimpse into Portland's past, with an eerie charm that's perfect for history buffs.

---

**Insider Tip:** Many Portland museums, including the Portland Museum of Art, offer free or discounted admission on select days. Check their websites for details.

---

## BUDGET-FRIENDLY EATERIES AND HAPPY HOUR DEALS

Portland's food scene may be renowned, but you don't need to splurge to enjoy a delicious meal.

- **Becky's Diner:** (390 Commercial St, Portland, ME | +1 207-773-7070) This waterfront diner is a local favorite for hearty breakfasts and comfort food at reasonable prices.
- **The Highroller Lobster Co.:** (104 Exchange St, Portland, ME | +1 207-536-1623) For an affordable take on Maine's iconic lobster roll, try The Highroller. Their customizable rolls start at a wallet-friendly price, with plenty of add-on options.
- **Slab Sicilian Street Food:** (25 Preble St, Portland, ME | +1 207-245-3088) Known for its massive Sicilian-style pizza slices,

Slab offers filling meals at a fraction of the cost of a sit-down restaurant.

- **Gilbert's Chowder House:** (92 Commercial St, Portland, ME | +1 207-871-5636) Grab a cup of clam chowder or a seafood stew without breaking the bank—perfect for a quick, satisfying meal.

## Happy Hour Finds:

- **Eventide Oyster Co.:** (86 Middle St, Portland, ME | +1 207-774-8538) Enjoy discounted oysters during happy hour at this popular spot.
- **Novare Res Bier Café:** (4 Canal Plaza, Portland, ME | +1 207-761-2437) A beer-lover's paradise with affordable happy hour specials and a cozy atmosphere.

---

**Fun Fact:** Many of Portland's breweries and food trucks offer pay-as-you-go options, so you can sample a variety of flavors without committing to a full meal.

---

## TIPS FOR AFFORDABLE ACCOMMODATIONS

Staying in Portland doesn't have to be expensive. With a little creativity, you can find options that fit your budget.

## Budget-Friendly Hotels:

- **Inn at St. John:** (939 Congress St, Portland, ME | +1 207-773-6481) This historic inn offers affordable rooms with charming decor and a convenient location.
- **Fireside Inn & Suites:** (81 Riverside St, Portland, ME | +1 207-774-5601) A great option for budget-conscious travelers, featuring comfortable rooms and free parking.
- **Vacation Rentals:** Websites like Airbnb and Vrbo offer a range of options, from private rooms to full apartments, often

at a lower cost than traditional hotels. Staying slightly outside downtown can save you even more.

**Hostels:**

- **Black Elephant Hostel:** (33 Hampshire St, Portland, ME | +1 207-712-7062) Perfect for solo travelers or those looking to meet fellow adventurers, this hostel offers dorm-style and private rooms at budget-friendly rates.

- **Insider Tip:** Visit during the shoulder seasons (late spring or early fall) for lower rates on accommodations and smaller crowds at popular attractions.

## GETTING AROUND PORTLAND ON A BUDGET

Portland is compact and walkable, making it easy to explore without spending much on transportation.

- **Walking and Biking:** Most of Portland's attractions are within walking distance, but for a quicker option, rent a bike from **Portland EnCYCLEpedia** (+1 207-774-9335).
- **Metro Bus Service:** The Greater Portland Metro Bus is an affordable way to get around the city and surrounding areas, with fares as low as $2. Consider the **METRO Breez** route for day trips to nearby towns like Freeport and Brunswick.
- **Casco Bay Lines:** For just a few dollars, you can take a ferry ride to one of the nearby Casco Bay islands—Peaks Island is a favorite for its quaint charm and scenic trails.

---

**Pro Tip:** Skip the rental car if you're staying downtown. Parking can be pricey, and public transportation or walking will get you to most places you want to see.

---

## HIDDEN GEMS FOR BUDGET TRAVELERS

- **Portland Farmers Market:** (Deering Oaks Park) A great place to sample local produce, baked goods, and crafts without spending much. You can even pack a picnic with your finds and enjoy it in the park.
- **Fort Gorges:** Accessible by kayak or a small boat, this historic fort is free to explore and offers stunning views of Casco Bay.
- **Western Promenade:** This quiet park in the West End is a peaceful retreat with sweeping views of the Fore River—and it's completely free.
- **Thompson's Point:** Many of the events at Thompson's Point, like outdoor concerts and art shows, have affordable or pay-what-you-can admission fees.

## TIPS FOR SAVING MONEY IN PORTLAND

- **Happy Hour Timing:** Plan your meals around happy hour to enjoy discounted food and drinks.
- **Free Activities:** Check local event listings for free happenings, like live music in parks or community festivals.
- **Bring Reusable Gear:** Pack a water bottle and reusable shopping bag to save on small but accumulating costs.

## EXPLORING WITHOUT SPLURGING

Portland proves that you don't need a big budget to enjoy a rich and fulfilling travel experience. From scenic parks and affordable eats to free events and cozy accommodations, this city offers plenty of ways to make your trip memorable without overspending. Up next, we'll dive into the high-end side of Portland, exploring luxurious experiences for travelers who want to indulge.

# 13

# LUXURY TRAVELERS

## INDULGE IN PORTLAND'S FINEST

Portland, Maine, may be known for its rugged coastlines and cozy charm, but it also caters to travelers who crave elegance and exclusivity. This city's luxury experiences combine world-class dining, private adventures, and upscale accommodations steeped in history. Whether you're sipping rare wines, sailing on a private yacht, or unwinding in a lavish spa, Portland offers a refined escape for those who seek the finer things in life.

## UPSCALE DINING AND FINE WINE TASTINGS

Portland's culinary scene doesn't just cater to foodies; it delivers unforgettable dining experiences that rival the world's top gastronomic destinations.

- **Fore Street:** (288 Fore St, Portland, ME | +1 207-775-2717) This James Beard Award-winning restaurant redefines rustic elegance with its wood-fired dishes and locally sourced ingredients. Request a table near the open kitchen for a front-row view of culinary artistry.

- **Twelve:** (115 Thames St, Portland, ME | +1 207-956-7174) Set in a sleek, modern building with views of the waterfront, Twelve offers a seasonal tasting menu that is as artful as it is delicious.
- **Central Provisions:** (414 Fore St, Portland, ME | +1 207-805-1085) This intimate restaurant serves inventive small plates that blend global influences with Maine's fresh ingredients.

## Fine Wine Tastings

- **Cellardoor at the Point:** (4 Thompsons Point, Portland, ME | +1 207-536-7700) This urban winery offers curated wine tastings in an elegant setting. Pair your glass with artisanal charcuterie for the full experience.
- **Old Port Wine and Cigar Shop:** (223 Commercial St, Portland, ME | +1 207-772-9463) For connoisseurs, this boutique shop hosts exclusive wine tastings featuring rare vintages and expert guidance.

---

**Hidden Knowledge:** Did you know Maine's cold climate is perfect for ice wine production? This rare dessert wine, made from frozen grapes, offers a sweet and complex flavor profile and is featured in tastings at select local wineries.

---

## EXCLUSIVE EXPERIENCES

Portland offers unique activities designed to elevate your visit into something truly extraordinary.

**Private Yacht Charters**

- **Casco Bay Custom Charters:** (+1 207-205-5796) Charter a private yacht to explore Casco Bay's secluded islands. Choose from custom experiences, like champagne brunch on the water or a sunset cruise with a personal chef.

- **Portland Schooner Co.:** (56 Commercial St, Portland, ME | +1 207-766-2500) Book a private sailing trip aboard a vintage schooner for a romantic and timeless maritime adventure.

---

**Fun Fact:** Many of Casco Bay's islands, like Great Diamond Island, were once exclusive summer retreats for the wealthy, complete with grand mansions and private clubs.

---

## Luxury Tours

- **Maine Foodie Tours: Elite Edition:** For an elevated culinary experience, Maine Foodie Tours offers private guided tastings at high-end restaurants, breweries, and bakeries tailored to your preferences.
- **Personalized Art Walks:** Hire a private guide to explore Portland's galleries, murals, and installations with behind-the-scenes insights from local artists.

## Spa Packages

- **Nine Stones Spa:** (185 Fore St, Portland, ME | +1 207-772-8480) This tranquil spa specializes in bespoke treatments, including luxury facials, hot stone massages, and full-day wellness packages.
- **The Spa at Cliff House Maine:** (591 Shore Rd, Cape Neddick, ME | +1 207-361-1000) Located just a short drive from Portland, this oceanfront spa offers a full range of treatments with breathtaking views of the Atlantic.

**Personal Anecdote:** My visit to Nine Stones Spa included a personalized aromatherapy massage. As the therapist worked out every knot, the blend of essential oils and serene atmosphere felt like a complete reset for my body and mind.

## HIGH-END BOUTIQUE HOTELS AND HISTORIC INNS

Portland's accommodations provide more than just a place to rest—they offer a luxurious retreat where every detail is designed to delight.

**Boutique Hotels**

- **The Press Hotel:** (119 Exchange St, Portland, ME | +1 207-808-8800) Housed in the former headquarters of a newspaper, The Press Hotel combines historic charm with modern luxury. The rooms feature vintage-inspired furnishings, and the on-site restaurant, UNION, is a destination in itself.
- **Canopy by Hilton Portland Waterfront:** (9 Center St, Portland, ME | +1 207-707-7200) This sleek hotel boasts stunning harbor views, plush accommodations, and a rooftop bar perfect for sunset cocktails.

**Historic Inns**

- **Blind Tiger:** (163 Danforth St, Portland, ME | +1 207-536-0415) This elegant inn blends 19th-century architecture with contemporary style. Each room is uniquely designed, offering an intimate and luxurious stay.
- **The Chadwick Bed & Breakfast:** (140 Chadwick St, Portland, ME | +1 207-774-5141) This beautifully restored Victorian home features upscale amenities like gourmet breakfasts and spa-like bathrooms.

**Trivia:** Blind Tiger's building once hosted extravagant Prohibition-era parties, earning it a reputation as a hub of old-world luxury.

## Hidden Gems for Luxury Travelers

- **Private Art Commissions:** Many of Portland's galleries, like **Art Collector Maine** (62 Exchange St, Portland, ME | +1 207-808-8184), offer opportunities to commission bespoke works from local artists—a unique way to bring a piece of Portland home.
- **Hidden Cellars:** Some of Portland's high-end restaurants, like Fore Street, offer private wine cellar dining experiences for an intimate and exclusive meal.
- **Scarborough Beach State Park:** (Scarborough, ME) For those seeking a quieter coastal escape, Scarborough Beach offers pristine sands and private cabana rentals during the summer months.

**Insider Tip:** Ask your hotel concierge about off-menu perks like private gallery tours, exclusive tasting menus, or secret happy hour spots reserved for locals in the know.

## TIPS FOR LUXURY TRAVELERS

- **Book Ahead:** Portland's luxury experiences often fill up quickly, especially during peak seasons. Reserve your dining, spa treatments, and private tours well in advance.
- **Seasonal Splurges:** Visit during fall for foliage-themed yacht charters or winter for cozy, exclusive spa retreats.
- **Personalized Itineraries:** Many boutique hotels and tour operators can curate bespoke itineraries to suit your

preferences.

## A TASTE OF ELEGANCE

Portland's blend of sophistication and charm makes it a dream destination for luxury travelers. Whether you're savoring fine wines, sailing through Casco Bay, or unwinding in a world-class spa, every moment feels indulgent. As we move forward, we'll explore Portland's welcoming atmosphere for LGBTQ+ travelers, highlighting its inclusive spaces and vibrant community.

## A TASTE OF ELEGANCE

# 14

# REMOTE WORKERS AND DIGITAL NOMADS

## WORK MEETS WANDERLUST

Imagine starting your day with freshly brewed coffee in a cozy café, working from a laptop with ocean views, and breaking up your afternoon with a stroll along cobblestone streets or a kayak trip in Casco Bay. Portland, Maine, is more than just a tourist destination—it's a haven for remote workers and digital nomads seeking a balance between productivity and adventure. With strong Wi-Fi, welcoming spaces, and a wealth of activities to recharge your mind, Portland makes working remotely feel like an indulgence.

## CAFÉS WITH STRONG WI-FI AND INSPIRING VIBES

Portland's café culture is perfect for remote workers who thrive in a cozy yet dynamic environment.

- **Tandem Coffee Roasters:** (742 Congress St, Portland, ME | +1 207-805-1887) Known for its excellent coffee and friendly atmosphere, Tandem offers plenty of seating and a relaxed vibe that's great for working.

- **Bard Coffee:** (185 Middle St, Portland, ME | +1 207-899-4788) This downtown hotspot is a favorite for its artisanal brews and strong Wi-Fi. Grab a seat by the large windows for plenty of natural light and great people-watching.
- **Coffee By Design:** (1 Diamond St, Portland, ME | +1 207-780-6767) With multiple locations around the city, this Portland staple combines excellent coffee with a quiet, productive environment. The East Bayside location has ample space for setting up shop.

---

**Hidden Tip:** Many Portland cafés roast their own beans, so you're guaranteed a high-quality cup of coffee. Bring your own mug—some spots offer discounts for eco-conscious patrons.

---

## COWORKING SPACES FOR SERIOUS PRODUCTIVITY

For those who need a dedicated workspace, Portland's coworking spaces offer all the amenities of an office with the flexibility remote workers love.

- **Cloudport CoWorking Multispace:** (63 Federal St, Portland, ME | +1 207-536-1357) Located downtown, Cloudport offers flexible memberships, private offices, and a welcoming community of entrepreneurs and remote workers.
- **KinoTek CoWorking:** (380 Cumberland Ave, Portland, ME | +1 207-222-7710) This sleek, modern coworking space is perfect for creatives and tech professionals, with fast Wi-Fi, ergonomic seating, and plenty of natural light.
- **SoPoCoWorks:** (1486 Broadway, South Portland, ME | +1 207-303-0615) Just across the bridge in South Portland, this space offers a quieter environment with a focus on community-driven workspaces.

> **Insider Tip:** Many coworking spaces in Portland offer day passes, so you can test out a few before committing to a membership.

## LONG-TERM STAY RECOMMENDATIONS FOR REMOTE WORK HUBS

Portland's accommodations cater to remote workers looking for longer stays, with options that combine comfort, convenience, and affordability.

### Hotels with Extended Stay Options

- **Residence Inn Portland Downtown/Waterfront:** (145 Fore St, Portland, ME | +1 207-761-1660) This hotel offers apartment-style suites with kitchenettes and workspaces, perfect for longer stays.
- **AC Hotel by Marriott Portland Downtown:** (158 Fore St, Portland, ME | +1 207-747-1640) With modern amenities and a prime location near the waterfront, this hotel caters to travelers balancing work and leisure.

### Vacation Rentals

Platforms like Airbnb and Vrbo offer countless options for extended stays in Portland. Look for rentals in the West End or Munjoy Hill for quiet neighborhoods with easy access to downtown.

> **Fun Fact:** Many historic homes in Portland have been converted into stylish rentals, giving you the chance to stay in a beautifully restored Victorian or Craftsman home.

### Unique Stays

- **The Blind Tiger:** (163 Danforth St, Portland, ME | +1 207-536-0415) This boutique inn offers longer-stay packages for remote workers seeking a mix of luxury and functionality.

---

**Insider Tip:** Look for accommodations with kitchen access to save money by cooking your own meals—then splurge on occasional takeout from Portland's incredible food scene.

---

## BALANCING PRODUCTIVITY WITH LEISURE ACTIVITIES

Portland's compact size makes it easy to balance work and play.

### Morning Breaks

- Start your day with a brisk walk along the **Eastern Promenade** to clear your head and soak in the ocean views.
- Stop by the **Portland Farmers Market** (Deering Oaks Park, Wednesdays and Saturdays) for fresh produce or a quick snack to fuel your morning.

### Lunch Escapes

- **Duckfat:** (43 Middle St, Portland, ME | +1 207-774-8080) Grab a gourmet panini or their famous fries for a mid-day pick-me-up.
- **Rose Foods:** (428 Forest Ave, Portland, ME | +1 207-835-0991) This bagel shop is a favorite for its creative toppings and fast service.

### After-Work Adventures

- Rent a kayak from **Portland Paddle** (East End Beach | +1 207-370-9730) and explore Casco Bay. Even a short paddle offers a refreshing change of pace.

- Check out a brewery like **Bissell Brothers** (4 Thompson's Point, Portland, ME | +1 207-808-8258) for a well-earned craft beer at the end of your workday.

## Weekend Activities

- Take a ferry to **Peaks Island** for a day of biking and beachcombing.
- Explore the trails at **Mackworth Island** or **Bradbury Mountain State Park** for a rejuvenating hike.

---

**Personal Anecdote:** On a weekday, I found myself kayaking at sunset after a long day of meetings. The calm water and pastel skies felt like the perfect reward for a productive day.

---

## HIDDEN GEMS FOR REMOTE WORKERS

- **Portland Public Library:** (5 Monument Square, Portland, ME | +1 207-871-1700) The library offers free Wi-Fi, quiet study spaces, and a central location—perfect for digital nomads on a budget.
- **Congress Square Park:** A small urban oasis with tables and chairs, this park often hosts live music or food vendors, making it a great spot to work al fresco.
- **Greenlight Studio:** (49 Dartmouth St, Portland, ME | +1 207-899-1900) A co-working café with a playful twist—it's a family-friendly space with a focus on community.

---

**Fun Fact:** Portland has one of the fastest-growing remote worker communities in New England, driven by its mix of creative industries and high quality of life.

---

## TIPS FOR DIGITAL NOMADS

- **Connectivity:** Bring a portable Wi-Fi hotspot just in case. While Portland's internet is generally reliable, it's good to have a backup.
- **Local Networks:** Join meetups or co-working events to connect with other remote workers—Portland's creative community is incredibly welcoming.
- **Plan for Seasons:** Maine's weather can be unpredictable. In the cooler months, seek out cozy cafés with fireplaces or heated outdoor seating.

## WHERE WORK MEETS WONDER

Portland strikes the perfect balance between productivity and play, offering remote workers a chance to recharge while staying connected. Whether you're logging in from a charming café, wrapping up work with a coastal sunset, or discovering hidden gems during a weekend break, this city makes every workday feel like an adventure. Next, we'll explore Portland's inclusivity and vibrant culture in a chapter dedicated to LGBTQ+ travelers.

**15**

# LGBTQ+ TRAVELERS

## PORTLAND'S PRIDEFUL HEART

Portland, Maine, isn't just a coastal escape—it's a beacon of inclusivity and celebration for LGBTQ+ travelers. Known for its vibrant community and welcoming atmosphere, the city offers a unique blend of nightlife, culture, and safe spaces that invite visitors to celebrate who they are. Whether you're sipping cocktails at a cozy bar, enjoying a dazzling drag performance, or marching in the city's colorful Pride parade, Portland offers something special for everyone in the LGBTQ+ community.

## LGBTQ+-FRIENDLY NIGHTLIFE, BARS, AND DRAG SHOWS

Portland's nightlife scene is both lively and inclusive, featuring welcoming spaces where everyone can feel at ease.

### Bars and Lounges

- **Blackstones:** (6 Pine St, Portland, ME | +1 207-775-2885) This beloved gay bar is a cornerstone of Portland's LGBTQ+ nightlife. With a relaxed vibe, friendly patrons, and events like karaoke and trivia, it's perfect for starting a night out or settling in for casual fun.

- **Flask Lounge:** (117 Spring St, Portland, ME | +1 207-772-3122) Known for its inclusive atmosphere, Flask regularly hosts dance parties, LGBTQ+ fundraisers, and themed nights. It's one of the best spots in town to let loose and make connections.
- **The Snug Pub:** (223 Congress St, Portland, ME | +1 207-619-7888) While not exclusively LGBTQ+, this cozy Irish pub in the East End is known for its welcoming ambiance and is a favorite for relaxed evenings with friends.

**Drag Shows and Entertainment**

- **Drag Brunch at The Highroller Lobster Co.:** (104 Exchange St, Portland, ME | +1 207-536-1623) This lively event pairs creative lobster rolls with show-stopping performances from Maine's top drag queens.
- **Portland House of Music and Events:** (25 Temple St, Portland, ME | +1 207-805-0134) Hosting everything from drag shows to queer dance parties, this venue is a hub for LGBTQ+ entertainment.

---

**Fun Fact:** Portland's drag scene is known for its humor and creativity, with performers like Cherry Lemonade and Gigi Gabor bringing both glamour and laughs to every show.

**Insider Tip:** Keep an eye on local LGBTQ+ event listings, as pop-up parties and one-night-only drag shows are common in Portland.

---

## INCLUSIVE RESTAURANTS, EVENTS, AND CULTURAL HUBS

Portland's inclusive spirit extends to its food scene and cultural spaces, creating a sense of community wherever you go.

## Inclusive Dining Spots

- **Hot Suppa:** (703 Congress St, Portland, ME | +1 207-871-5005) Known for its welcoming atmosphere, this Southern-inspired spot is popular among LGBTQ+ locals. Their brunch, featuring classics like shrimp and grits, is a must-try.
- **Bao Bao Dumpling House:** (133 Spring St, Portland, ME | +1 207-772-8400) This stylish dumpling house is not only a local favorite but also a welcoming space for all. The cozy environment and delicious food make it perfect for casual dinners or first dates.
- **The Honey Paw:** (78 Middle St, Portland, ME | +1 207-774-8538) This modern Asian fusion spot is celebrated for its communal vibe, encouraging shared plates and conversation.

## Cultural Hubs and Annual Events

- **Equality Community Center:** (15 Casco St, Portland, ME | +1 207-518-0546) This LGBTQ+ hub hosts everything from educational workshops to art exhibits and social gatherings, creating a welcoming space for visitors and locals alike.
- **Queer Book Club at Longfellow Books:** (1 Monument Way, Portland, ME | +1 207-772-4045) This monthly meet-up celebrates LGBTQ+ authors and stories, offering a space to connect with fellow readers.
- **Maine Queer Film Festival:** Held annually, this festival showcases films that highlight LGBTQ+ stories and experiences, creating a platform for thought-provoking cinema.

---

**Personal Anecdote:** I stumbled upon a First Friday Art Walk showcasing work by LGBTQ+ artists in Congress Square Park. Watching drag performers and spoken word poets share their talents alongside vibrant art installations was a testament to Portland's celebration of creativity and diversity.

## ANNUAL PORTLAND PRIDE AND COMMUNITY RESOURCES

Pride in Portland is more than just a parade—it's a week-long celebration of love, acceptance, and visibility.

### Portland Pride Week Highlights

- **Pride Parade:** This vibrant event winds through downtown Portland, with floats, dancers, and marchers representing the diverse LGBTQ+ community. It's a joyous, colorful celebration that draws thousands of attendees each year.
- **Pride Festival at Deering Oaks Park:** After the parade, the festivities continue with live music, local vendors, and community organization booths. It's a family-friendly event that combines fun with advocacy.
- **Pride After-Parties:** Local bars and clubs, including Flask Lounge and Blackstones, host themed parties to cap off the day's celebrations.

### Community Resources

- **MaineTransNet:** A nonprofit supporting transgender individuals through peer support and advocacy.
- **Out Maine:** Focused on supporting LGBTQ+ youth, this organization provides resources and programming for young people across the state.
- **Portland Outright:** Dedicated to queer and trans youth, this group fosters empowerment and activism through workshops and events.

---

**Hidden Knowledge:** Portland's first Pride Parade in 1987 featured just a few dozen marchers. Today, the event has grown into one of New England's largest Pride celebrations, reflecting the city's unwavering support for LGBTQ+ rights.

## HIDDEN GEMS FOR LGBTQ+ TRAVELERS

- **Rising Tide Brewing Company:** (103 Fox St, Portland, ME | +1 207-370-2337) This brewery regularly partners with LGBTQ+ organizations for events, making it a welcoming space for the community.
- **Nonesuch River Brewing:** (201 Gorham Rd, Scarborough, ME | +1 207-219-8948) Located just outside Portland, this brewery has hosted LGBTQ+ nights in partnership with local groups, offering a relaxed vibe and great craft beer.
- **Portland Harbor Hotel Courtyard:** (468 Fore St, Portland, ME | +1 207-775-9090) This hidden oasis in the heart of downtown features a lush outdoor courtyard—perfect for a quiet moment amidst the city's bustle.

**Fun Fact:** Portland is home to one of the few LGBTQ+-focused sailing groups in New England. Look into events hosted by local sailing clubs for unique opportunities to meet other travelers and locals.

## TIPS FOR LGBTQ+ TRAVELERS

- **Use Social Media:** Follow local LGBTQ+ organizations like EqualityMaine for updates on events and resources during your visit.
- **Connect with Locals:** Portland's LGBTQ+ residents are incredibly friendly and often eager to share recommendations or stories about the city's vibrant community.
- **Stay Safe:** While Portland is very welcoming, it's always good to stay aware of your surroundings when exploring at night or attending large events.

## A CITY THAT CELEBRATES DIVERSITY

Portland's commitment to inclusivity and celebration makes it a standout destination for LGBTQ+ travelers. From vibrant nightlife to meaningful cultural events, this city invites you to be yourself and find connection at every turn. As we look ahead, we'll explore how Portland transforms with the seasons, ensuring a unique experience no matter the time of year.

# 16

# SEASONAL VISITORS - HIGHLIGHTS FOR EVERY SEASON

## A CITY FOR ALL SEASONS

Portland, Maine, is a city that wears its seasons beautifully, offering something special no matter when you visit. While Chapter 3 highlighted iconic seasonal activities like holiday lights, foliage tours, and summer festivals, this chapter dives deeper into the experiences that make each season unique. From hidden gems and insider tips to under-the-radar events and natural wonders, this chapter is your guide to embracing the best of Portland year-round.

## SUMMER: BEYOND THE SUNSHINE

Summer in Portland is a season of vibrancy, with long, warm days inviting you to explore the coastline, enjoy outdoor dining, and partake in local traditions.

### Hidden Coastal Gems

- **Fort Gorges:** Accessible only by kayak or small boat, this granite fort offers an adventure off the beaten path. Rent a kayak from **Portland Paddle** (East End Beach, Portland, ME

| +1 207-370-9730) to paddle out and explore its moss-covered halls and panoramic views of Casco Bay.

- **Secluded Beaches:** While Willard Beach and East End Beach are well-known, take a drive to **Crescent Beach State Park** (109 Bowery Beach Rd, Cape Elizabeth, ME | +1 207-799-5871) for a quieter seaside escape.

**Local Summer Traditions**

- **Clambakes on Peaks Island:** Join a classic New England clambake hosted by locals or tour companies, where you'll enjoy lobster, clams, and corn on a private beach. Peaks Island's quaint charm and friendly community make it the perfect summer getaway.
- **Puffin Watching:** Book a wildlife cruise to Eastern Egg Rock or Machias Seal Island to spot puffins in their breeding grounds. These colorful seabirds are only in Maine during summer.

---

**Trivia:** Did you know that Portland's Casco Bay is home to more than 200 islands, often referred to as the "Calendar Islands," because you could theoretically explore one for every day of the year?

---

## FALL: NEW PERSPECTIVES ON FOLIAGE AND FESTIVALS

Autumn in Maine is celebrated for its fiery foliage, but there's much more to explore than just the leaves.

**Expanding Fall Foliage Experiences**

- **Apple Orchards and Corn Mazes:** Visit **Libby & Son U-Picks** (86 Sawyer Mountain Rd, Limerick, ME | +1 207-793-4749) for apple picking, hayrides, and fresh cider donuts. It's a quintessential Maine experience with a family-friendly vibe.

- **Rooftop Views:** For a unique perspective on the fall colors, head to **Luna Rooftop Bar** (Canopy by Hilton Portland Waterfront, 9 Center St, Portland, ME | +1 207-707-7200) and sip a seasonal cocktail while gazing out over the treetops and harbor.

## Festivals with a Local Flair

- **Freeport Fall Festival:** Just a short drive from Portland, this arts and crafts festival features live music, local vendors, and food stalls in a festive village atmosphere.
- **Harvest on the Harbor:** This upscale food festival celebrates Maine's culinary scene with tastings of everything from craft beer to oysters.

---

**Insider Tip:** Combine a fall foliage drive with a stop at **Hacker's Hill Preserve** (Quaker Ridge Rd, Casco, ME). This little-known viewpoint offers stunning panoramas of Sebago Lake and the White Mountains.

---

# WINTER: MORE THAN JUST COZY CORNERS

While Portland's fireplaces and holiday decorations are iconic, there's a whole world of winter wonder waiting to be uncovered.

## Outdoor Winter Adventures

- **Ice Skating at Thompson's Point:** (10 Thompson's Point Rd, Portland, ME) The **Rink at Thompson's Point** transforms this riverside location into a magical ice-skating venue, complete with fire pits and a hot cocoa bar.
- **Winter Birding at Scarborough Marsh:** (92 Pine Point Rd, Scarborough, ME | +1 207-883-5100) Winter may seem an unusual time for birdwatching, but Scarborough Marsh comes alive with waterfowl and rare overwintering species.

## Winter Markets and Celebrations

- **Flavors of Winter Market:** Located in East Bayside, this indoor market showcases local makers, bakers, and artisans, offering a festive alternative to traditional holiday shopping.
- **Victorian Christmas Events:** While Chapter 3 touched on the Victorian Mansion's holiday decor, another hidden gem is the **Portland Symphony Orchestra's Magic of Christmas** performance, which blends music, storytelling, and tradition in a magical seasonal event.

---

**Fun Fact:** Maine's longest season is winter, often lasting up to five months. Portland's locals embrace it with outdoor activities and cozy indoor traditions to stave off cabin fever.

---

## SPRING: RENEWAL AND HIDDEN BLOOMS

Spring in Portland is a season of rebirth, when gardens bloom, and local farms burst into activity.

### Gardens Beyond the Usual

- **Tate House Museum Herb Garden:** (1270 Westbrook St, Portland, ME | +1 207-774-6177) This historic home's garden features medicinal and culinary herbs that were commonly used in the 18th century. Tours combine history with horticulture for a unique spring outing.
- **Wildflower Walks:** Visit **Clifford Park** (South St, Biddeford, ME | +1 207-282-4167) for trails dotted with native wildflowers, a hidden gem for nature lovers.

### Local Farms and Farmers Markets

- **Spring Lambing at Wolfe's Neck Center:** (184 Burnett Rd, Freeport, ME | +1 207-865-4469) Spring marks lambing season at this coastal farm, where visitors can meet baby animals and learn about sustainable farming practices.

- **Portland Winter Farmers Market Transition:** As spring arrives, the market moves from its winter indoor location back to **Deering Oaks Park,** filling the city with vibrant colors and fresh produce.

---

**Trivia:** Maine's state flower is the white pine cone and tassel—a nod to the state's nickname as the "Pine Tree State." Spring is the best time to spot its fresh growth.

---

## BUILDING ON SEASONAL THEMES FROM CHAPTER 3

While Chapter 3 introduced seasonal highlights, this chapter dives deeper into hidden spots, local traditions, and fresh perspectives that offer a richer understanding of Portland's seasonal charm. For example:

- Instead of repeating "holiday lights" from Chapter 3, here we highlight **The Rink at Thompson's Point** and **Magic of Christmas**, adding variety to winter offerings.
- Spring builds on farmers markets but introduces lesser-known locations like Wolfe's Neck for unique animal encounters.
- Summer expands into the exploration of **lesser-visited islands** and local clambakes, offering depth beyond harbor cruises.

## TIPS FOR SEASONAL VISITORS

- **Bundle Up for Winter:** Layers are key for winter travelers, especially if you plan on enjoying outdoor adventures like snowshoeing or skating.
- **Plan for Mud Season:** Early spring, known as "mud season," can be a little messy—pack sturdy shoes for trails and parks.

- **Make Reservations:** Fall foliage season and summer festivals are busy times—book accommodations and activities early.

## PORTLAND'S EVER-CHANGING CANVAS

Portland is a city where the seasons truly shape your experience. Whether you're chasing the golden light of fall, enjoying a clambake on a summer island, or cozying up by a winter fireplace, each season offers its own rewards. Next, we'll provide practical tips for planning your Portland adventure, ensuring you have everything you need to make the most of your time in this ever-changing city.

## PART 3: HIDDEN GEMS

Portland, Maine, is a city of contrasts—its beauty is as much in what you see as in what lies hidden. While its iconic lighthouses and bustling Old Port draw thousands of visitors, its secrets are what linger with those who take the time to uncover them. This part of the guidebook delves into the mysterious, the hidden, and the delightfully unexpected. From secret gardens and trails to speakeasies and shipwrecks, this is where Portland reveals its soul. Let's explore the chapters that will take you deep into its heart.

**17**

# PORTLAND'S HIDDEN HISTORY AND SECRET SPOTS

## A CITY BUILT ON SECRETS

Every city has its secrets, but in Portland, they seem to rise from the cobblestones themselves. Beneath the charming façade of boutique shops and bustling wharfs lies a network of untold stories—whispers of rum-runners, ghostly figures, and hidden passageways that have survived the tides of time. This chapter invites you to step off the beaten path and into a world of intrigue, where the city's history comes alive in its hidden corners.

## UNDER-THE-RADAR SPOTS AND FORGOTTEN HISTORIES

### Fort Gorges

- **Where:** Casco Bay (Accessible by kayak or private boat).
- **The Story:** Fort Gorges rises from the waters of Casco Bay like a scene out of a Gothic novel. Built during the Civil War, it never saw combat and has since been left to the elements, transforming into a moss-covered relic. Its eerie tunnels and

crumbling walls feel untouched by time, and the rooftop offers sweeping views of the bay.

---

**Anecdote:** Local kayakers often speak of hearing strange noises —footsteps echoing through the tunnels, whispers in the wind. Legend has it that the spirits of soldiers who never saw battle still linger here, pacing the ramparts.

**Tip:** Rent a kayak from Portland Paddle (East End Beach, Portland) and explore the fort in the early morning when the light is soft and the bay is quiet. Bring a flashlight for the dark passageways.

---

## Battery Steele on Peaks Island

- **Where:** Peaks Island, Casco Bay.
- **The Story:** A relic of World War II, Battery Steele is now a canvas for artists and a playground for adventurers. The sprawling bunkers are adorned with graffiti, each piece adding new life to its weathered concrete walls. The stark beauty of the site and the vibrancy of the artwork make it a must-visit for those who crave the unexpected.

---

**Local Legend:** Locals speak of a ghostly soldier who roams the battery at dusk. Known as the "Soldier of Steele," his footsteps are said to echo through the tunnels when the island grows quiet.

**Tip:** Visit at sunrise or sunset to enjoy dramatic lighting and solitude. Wear sturdy shoes for exploring uneven terrain.

---

## The Secret Tunnel System

- **Where:** Beneath the Old Port, Portland.

- **The Story:** Rumored to stretch beneath the Old Port, these tunnels are said to have been used for everything from smuggling rum during Prohibition to Shanghaiing sailors in the 19th century. Though many of the entrances are sealed, their existence has fueled countless stories.

**Anecdote:** During renovations, a bar owner stumbled upon a bricked-up passageway filled with vintage liquor bottles. While the tunnel was impassable, it offered a tantalizing glimpse into Portland's clandestine past.

**Tip:** Join a ghost or history tour to hear firsthand accounts of these hidden passageways. Some guides even share maps of where the tunnels might be.

## Spring Point Ledge Lighthouse Interior Tours

- **Where:** South Portland.
- **The Story:** This iconic lighthouse stands at the end of a breakwater, its beacon a testament to the seafarers who navigated these waters. On rare summer weekends, visitors can climb its spiral staircase and see the inner workings of a lighthouse while enjoying panoramic views of Casco Bay.

**Fun Fact:** The granite breakwater connecting the lighthouse to the mainland was added to protect the lighthouse, making the journey to it an adventure in itself.

**Tip:** Time your visit during one of the summer open houses to access the interior.

## The Wreck of the Annie C. Maguire

- **Where:** Portland Head Light, Cape Elizabeth.
- **The Story:** On Christmas Eve in 1886, the schooner Annie C. Maguire wrecked just offshore. Though the crew was saved, the story remains a mystery—how could an experienced captain crash into such well-known rocks? Visitors say they've seen ghostly lights on foggy nights, perhaps the spirits of sailors searching for safe passage.

---

**Tip:** Visit on a misty day to soak in the eerie atmosphere of this storied spot.

---

## QUIRKY MUSEUMS AND HISTORIC FINDS

### The Observatory's Secret Spiral Staircase

- **Where:** 138 Congress St, Portland.
- **The Story:** The Portland Observatory isn't for stargazing—it's a maritime signal tower dating back to 1807. Its spiral staircase, crafted entirely from wood, is a masterpiece of engineering. Climbing to the top provides unparalleled views of the harbor and skyline.

---

**Insider Insight:** Guides often share how merchants relied on the Observatory to identify incoming ships, a system that predates modern communication.

---

### The Victoria Mansion Basement

- **Where:** 109 Danforth St, Portland.
- **The Story:** Beneath the grandeur of the Victoria Mansion lies its often-overlooked basement. This space, which housed the mansion's original heating system and servant quarters, is a

fascinating glimpse into 19th-century life. Occasionally featured in special tours, it's a treasure trove of historical tools and artifacts.

---

**Fun Fact:** The basement's architecture features elements of the original construction, including wooden beams and brickwork that have stood the test of time.

**Tip:** Keep an eye out for special "behind-the-scenes" tours, which occasionally include access to this hidden area.

---

## International Cryptozoology Museum

- **Where:** 4 Thompson's Point, Portland.
- **The Story:** This one-of-a-kind museum celebrates the world of mythical creatures, from Bigfoot to Nessie. It's a fascinating blend of science, folklore, and imagination.

---

**Fun Fact:** Founder Loren Coleman is a leading cryptozoologist who has spent decades collecting artifacts and stories from around the world.

---

## Umbrella Cover Museum

- **Where:** Peaks Island.
- **The Story:** This museum holds the Guinness World Record for the largest collection of umbrella covers. It's quirky, unexpected, and full of charm. The owner's humor and enthusiasm make every visit delightful.

## SHOPPING FOR UNIQUE TREASURES

### Portland Flea-for-All

- **Where:** 585 Congress St, Portland.
- **The Story:** A vintage lover's paradise, this marketplace is filled with treasures ranging from retro furniture to handmade crafts. Vendors are often local artisans who love to share the stories behind their goods.

### Green Hand Bookshop

- **Where:** 661 Congress St, Portland.
- **The Story:** Specializing in rare and second-hand books, this shop is perfect for anyone seeking unique finds. It's also a haven for those interested in Maine's ghost stories and maritime legends.

### Material Objects

- **Where:** 500 Congress St, Portland.
- **The Story:** Material Objects is a quirky boutique filled with vintage clothing, eclectic accessories, and treasures from bygone eras. It's a place where fashion meets nostalgia, offering everything from retro gowns to antique jewelry. Its cozy, labyrinth-like layout makes every visit feel like a treasure hunt.

---

**Fun Fact:** The boutique's owner is a Portland native who curates items based on stories they carry, often with ties to Maine's past.

**Tip:** Ask the staff about the history of some of their most unique pieces—they're often happy to share fascinating tidbits.

---

## NATURE'S SECRETS AWAIT

History holds the stories of Portland's past, but its natural landscapes whisper a different kind of secret—one of beauty, solitude, and adventure. As we leave behind the city's mysterious tunnels and forgotten shipwrecks, let's journey into its tranquil gardens, secluded beaches, and hidden trails in Chapter 18: Natural Wonders and Hidden Adventures.

## 18

# NATURAL WONDERS AND HIDDEN ADVENTURES

## DISCOVER NATURE'S HIDDEN GEMS

Maine is celebrated for its rugged coastlines and sprawling forests, but even here, some treasures remain hidden. In Portland and its surroundings, secret gardens bloom quietly, waterfalls whisper their songs to those who find them, and trails lead to places that feel untouched by time. This chapter is your guide to the natural side of Portland that only the curious traveler will discover.

## SECRET GARDENS AND NATURAL ESCAPES

### The Rose Garden in Deering Oaks Park

- **Where:** Deering Oaks Park, Portland.
- **The Story:** Nestled in a quiet corner of this historic park, the Rose Garden bursts into bloom every summer, filling the air with the heady scent of heirloom roses. Its charm lies in its sense of seclusion—though the park is often busy, the garden feels like a secret haven.

**Tip:** Visit in early June for peak blooms, and bring a book or a journal to enjoy in the garden's peaceful atmosphere.

---

## Longfellow Garden

- **Where:** Wadsworth-Longfellow House, 489 Congress St, Portland.
- **The Story:** Tucked behind the historic Wadsworth-Longfellow House, this Colonial Revival garden is a quiet sanctuary in the middle of the city. Its neatly arranged flowerbeds and shaded benches offer a serene escape from the bustle of Congress Street.

---

**Fun Fact:** The garden is maintained to reflect the styles popular during Henry Wadsworth Longfellow's era, making it as much a historical artifact as a place of beauty.

**Tip:** Pair your visit with a tour of the Longfellow House for a complete historical experience.

---

## Jewell Falls

- **Where:** Fore River Sanctuary, Portland.
- **The Story:** Portland's only natural waterfall is a hidden treasure surrounded by a forested preserve. Its gentle cascade and the soft rustle of leaves make it the perfect spot for quiet reflection. The nearby trails wind through wetlands and offer a glimpse of local wildlife, including herons and foxes.

---

**Tip:** Head to Jewell Falls in the spring, when the snowmelt makes the waterfall especially lively.

---

## Hidden Lagoon on Mackworth Island

- **Where:** Mackworth Island, Falmouth.
- **The Story:** Off the main trail on Mackworth Island lies a hidden lagoon, its glassy waters reflecting the trees and sky. This secluded spot feels like a scene out of a fairy tale, especially during golden hour when the sunlight dapples the water.

**Tip:** Look for the whimsical fairy houses scattered along the trails, built by visitors who couldn't resist adding a touch of magic.

## Hamilton House Gardens

- **Where:** 40 Vaughans Ln, South Berwick, ME.
- **The Story:** Surrounding the historic Hamilton House are stunning Colonial Revival gardens that overlook the Salmon Falls River. The gardens feature elegant walkways, vibrant flower beds, and antique statues, creating a sense of timeless beauty.

**Fun Fact:** The Hamilton House itself was built in 1785 and is part of the National Historic Register, making it a perfect pairing for history and garden lovers alike.

**Tip:** Visit in late spring when the gardens are in full bloom. Consider packing a picnic to enjoy on the lawn.

## HIDDEN BEACHES AND COASTAL ESCAPES

### Seawall Beach

- **Where:** Phippsburg, ME.

- **The Story:** This pristine beach is accessible only via a mile-long hike through Morse Mountain Preserve, ensuring it remains quiet and untouched. The reward for the walk is a wide expanse of soft sand and crashing waves, perfect for a peaceful escape.

---

**Tip:** Visit during low tide to explore the tidal pools that teem with marine life, from tiny crabs to starfish.

---

## Kettle Cove

- **Where:** Cape Elizabeth, ME.
- **The Story:** Often overlooked in favor of the nearby Crescent Beach, Kettle Cove is a hidden gem where tidal pools glimmer in the sunlight, and fishing boats dot the horizon. Its tranquil beauty makes it a favorite for locals looking to avoid the crowds.

---

**Tip:** Pack a picnic and stay for sunset, when the cove glows with golden light.

---

## Ferry Beach Hidden Cove

- **Where:** Ferry Beach State Park, Saco, ME.
- **The Story:** Tucked away from the more frequented areas of Ferry Beach is a secluded cove that feels like a private oasis. Surrounded by lush greenery and soft sands, it's a perfect spot for quiet reflection or a romantic escape.

---

**Tip:** Visit early in the morning to enjoy the cove when it's at its quietest. Bring a towel and a book—it's the ideal place to while away a few peaceful hours.

## Higgins Beach Shipwreck

- **Where:** Higgins Beach, Scarborough, ME.
- **The Story:** At low tide, the skeletal remains of an old shipwreck emerge from the sands at Higgins Beach. The ship, believed to date back over a century, adds a hauntingly beautiful element to the already picturesque setting.

**Fun Fact:** The wreck's exact history remains a mystery, but it's a favorite spot for photographers and history buffs alike.

**Tip:** Check tide schedules to ensure you visit when the wreck is visible.

# HIDDEN TRAILS AND OUTDOOR ADVENTURES

## Cliff Walk at Prouts Neck

- **Where:** Scarborough, ME.
- **The Story:** This coastal trail winds along dramatic cliffs, offering breathtaking views of the Atlantic and the rocky shoreline. Accessible to the public but often uncrowded, it feels like a secret path to another world.

**Tip:** Sunrise here is spectacular, with the light illuminating the rugged cliffs and ocean waves.

## The Labyrinth at Pownalborough Court House

- **Where:** Dresden, ME.

- **The Story:** Tucked behind a historic courthouse, this meditative labyrinth is a hidden treasure surrounded by whispering pines. Walking its winding paths is a tranquil experience that invites reflection and mindfulness.

---

Tip: Combine your visit with a tour of the courthouse for a deeper dive into local history.

---

## The Enchanted Forest Trail

- **Where:** Brunswick, ME.
- **The Story:** This magical trail winds through a dense forest dotted with whimsical fairy houses and tiny sculptures crafted by local artists and visitors alike. The trail's quiet beauty and creative touches make it feel like stepping into a storybook.

---

Fun Fact: The fairy houses are constantly changing as visitors leave their own imaginative creations behind, ensuring no two visits are ever the same.

Tip: Bring a small natural item—like a shell or a twig—to add your own touch to the trail's fairy kingdom.

---

## The Desert of Maine

- **Where:** 95 Desert Rd, Freeport, ME.
- **The Story:** A geological anomaly, the Desert of Maine features 40 acres of natural sand dunes surrounded by lush forest. Once farmland, the site became "desert" due to soil erosion, creating a unique and fascinating landscape. Visitors can explore walking trails and learn about its unusual history at the visitor center.

---

**Fun Fact:** The site's original farmhouse still stands and serves as a museum dedicated to the land's transformation.

**Tip:** Take a guided tour to hear the full story of how the desert came to be—it's as intriguing as the landscape itself.

## The Marginal Way

- **Where:** Ogunquit, ME.
- **The Story:** This scenic coastal walkway spans over a mile, offering breathtaking views of rocky cliffs, crashing waves, and the open Atlantic. Though popular, there are quieter pockets along the way that feel like your own private slice of Maine's coastline.

**Tip:** Visit at sunrise or sunset for the most spectacular views. Bring a camera—the photo opportunities are endless.

## A DIFFERENT KIND OF ADVENTURE

Portland's natural escapes bring peace to the soul, but as the sun sets, a different energy takes hold of the city. In the next chapter, we'll uncover Portland's secret speakeasies, hidden lounges, and offbeat after-dark activities that promise excitement and intrigue in Chapter 19: Secret Bars, Speakeasies, and Hidden Activities.

19

# SECRET BARS, SPEAKEASIES, AND HIDDEN ACTIVITIES

## A CITY THAT COMES ALIVE AFTER DARK

When night falls in Portland, the city transforms. Hidden behind unmarked doors and tucked into historic basements are bars and lounges that evoke a sense of mystery and exclusivity. Here, cocktails are served with a touch of intrigue, and every show or secret activity feels like you've stumbled onto something extraordinary. This chapter will guide you to Portland's after-dark treasures, where the real magic begins.

## SECRET BARS AND SPEAKEASIES

### Lincoln's

- **Where:** 36 Market St, Portland.
- **The Story:** Hidden behind an unmarked door, this speakeasy is a local favorite. Named after the $5 bill, which graces the bar's decor, it offers reasonably priced cocktails in a cozy, candlelit atmosphere.

**Tip:** Look for the subtle sign hinting at the entrance—it's easy to miss but part of the charm.

---

## Bramhall Pub

- **Where:** 769 Congress St, Portland.
- **The Story:** Tucked into a historic basement, this Prohibition-style pub combines stone walls, dim lighting, and craft cocktails to create an intimate, old-world ambiance. Its underground vibe makes it feel like a well-kept secret.

---

**Tip:** Try their house-made sangria or ask the bartender for seasonal cocktail specials.

---

## The Jewel Box

- **Where:** 644 Congress St, Portland.
- **The Story:** This whimsical cocktail bar takes mixology to an art form, crafting drinks that are as visually stunning as they are delicious. The intimate setting makes it perfect for a quiet evening.

---

**Tip:** Ask about the bartender's "off-menu" creations for a truly unique experience.

---

## Batson River Brewing & Distilling: Secret Upstairs Lounge

- **Where:** 82 Hanover St, Portland.
- **The Story:** While Batson River is known for its craft brews and spirits, few visitors know about its intimate upstairs lounge. Accessed via a discreet staircase, this cozy space feels

like a private club, complete with plush seating, dim lighting, and an exclusive cocktail menu.

**Tip:** Ask the bartender about the upstairs lounge when ordering —they'll direct you to the staircase if it's open.

## The Blind Pig

- **Where:** 23 Wharf St, Portland.
- **The Story:** The Blind Pig is a speakeasy tucked away in Portland's Old Port. Its unmarked entrance adds an air of mystery, and its craft cocktails served in antique glassware, transport guests to the Prohibition era.

**Tip:** Look for the flickering lantern outside—that's your clue you've found the right place.

## HIDDEN ACTIVITIES AND UNIQUE EXPERIENCES

### Live Jazz at Blue

- **Where:** 650 Congress St, Portland.
- **The Story:** This cozy venue features intimate jazz performances and a rotating lineup of local and international musicians. The welcoming atmosphere makes every show feel like a private concert.

**Tip:** Arrive early to grab a good seat—the venue is small and fills up quickly.

## The Front Porch Piano Bar

- **Where:** 9 Shore Rd, Ogunquit, ME.
- **The Story:** This lively piano bar is a short drive from Portland but worth the trip. Known for its welcoming atmosphere and talented pianists, the bar encourages singalongs and late-night revelry.

**Tip:** Arrive early to grab a seat near the piano—it's the best spot for joining in the fun.

## The Apohadion Theater

- **Where:** 107 Hanover St, Portland.
- **The Story:** This intimate theater hosts indie films, live music, and avant-garde performances. Its eclectic schedule ensures there's always something unexpected happening.

**Tip:** Check their calendar for pop-up events and one-night-only performances.

## Silent Disco on the Promenade

- **Where:** Eastern Promenade, Portland.
- **The Story:** Every summer, the Eastern Promenade transforms into a dance floor for silent disco enthusiasts. Participants don wireless headphones and dance to curated playlists as the city skyline glows in the background.

**Tip:** Bring a friend or two—it's more fun when you have someone to share the surreal experience with.

## BEYOND THE CITY LIMITS

Portland's nightlife may be magnetic, but its surrounding areas hold adventures of their own. From charming coastal towns to breathtaking natural wonders, the next section explores the day trips and excursions that will take your Portland experience to the next level. Join us in ***Part 4: Day Trips and Excursions*** for a journey beyond the city's borders.

# PART 4: DAY TRIPS AND EXCURSIONS

## 20

# CASCO BAY ISLANDS

## A JOURNEY ACROSS THE BAY

The Casco Bay Islands are like a string of pearls scattered across the waters off Portland's coast—each one distinct yet collectively dazzling. Whether you're drawn to the historic remnants of a bygone era, the peaceful rhythm of island life, or the thrill of discovery, the islands offer a world of adventure just a short ferry ride away. From bustling Peaks Island to the tranquil shores of Cliff Island, Casco Bay is a treasure trove of experiences waiting to be uncovered.

## EXPLORING PEAKS ISLAND: THE GATEWAY TO CASCO BAY

**Where:** Accessible by ferry from the Casco Bay Lines terminal in Portland.

Peaks Island is often considered the most accessible and lively of the Casco Bay Islands. Known as the "Coney Island of Maine" in the late 19th century, it once hosted an amusement park, theaters, and grand hotels. Today, Peaks retains its charm with a mix of quiet residential streets, bustling shops, and scenic coastal views.

**The Experience:**

A day on Peaks Island offers something for everyone. Start your visit by renting a bike from **Brad's Bike Rental** (115 Island Ave, Peaks Island, ME 04108), located just steps from the ferry dock. Pedal your way around the island's four-mile perimeter road, which hugs the coastline and offers stunning views of Casco Bay. Along the way, you'll encounter hidden beaches, rocky outcroppings, and quaint cottages adorned with lobster traps and buoys.

One of Peaks' standout attractions is **Battery Steele**, a massive WWII-era fort now covered in vibrant graffiti. Its dark tunnels and echoing chambers invite exploration, while the surrounding trails lead to scenic vistas. Locals share tales of ghostly encounters at the battery, particularly on foggy evenings, adding an element of mystery to the experience.

For lunch, stop at **The Inn on Peaks Island** (33 Island Ave, Peaks Island, ME 04108), a charming spot offering fresh seafood and local brews. If you're craving something sweet, head to **Peaks Café** (50 Island Ave, Peaks Island, ME 04108) for homemade ice cream or a cup of locally roasted coffee.

---

**Insider Tip:** Time your visit to coincide with low tide, when hidden beaches emerge along the island's edges. These secluded spots are perfect for a quiet picnic or some shell collecting.

---

## GREAT DIAMOND ISLAND: A TRANQUIL RETREAT

**Where:** Accessible by ferry from Portland.

Once a military outpost during World War II, Great Diamond Island is now a haven for peace and relaxation. Its quiet beaches, historic ruins, and charming inns make it an ideal escape for those seeking solitude.

**The Experience:**

Great Diamond Island feels like stepping back in time. Its tree-lined paths and historic buildings evoke the island's past as Fort McKinley, a military base protecting Casco Bay. Today, many of the fort's barracks have been converted into private homes and vacation rentals, blending old-world charm with modern amenities.

Start your visit with a leisurely walk along Diamond Cove, a picturesque waterfront area dotted with shops, galleries, and cafés. **Diamond's Edge Restaurant** (16 Diamond Ave, Great Diamond Island, ME 04109) is a standout dining option, offering fresh seafood with views of the cove. Afterward, explore the island's trails, which wind through wooded areas and past the remnants of military bunkers.

---

**Fun Fact:** Great Diamond Island is car-free, adding to its serene atmosphere. Transportation is limited to bikes and golf carts, reinforcing the island's leisurely pace.

**Insider Tip:** Book a night at the Inn at Diamond Cove if your schedule allows. Staying overnight gives you a chance to enjoy the island's peace and quiet after the last ferry departs.

---

## CLIFF ISLAND: RUSTIC CHARM AT THE EDGE OF THE BAY

**Where:** The outermost island accessible by ferry from Portland.

For those seeking a true escape from modern life, Cliff Island is the perfect destination. With its unpaved roads, minimal development, and close-knit community, the island offers a glimpse into a simpler way of life.

**The Experience:**

Cliff Island's unspoiled beauty is its greatest draw. The lack of paved roads encourages exploration by foot or bike, and the island's small size makes it easy to navigate. Highlights include Fisherman's Point, a rocky promontory with sweeping views of Casco Bay, and the island's small general store, which serves as a hub for locals and visitors alike.

**Local Insight:** Residents of Cliff Island are fiercely protective of their island's charm and traditions. Visitors are welcomed with open arms but are encouraged to respect the island's quiet lifestyle.

**Insider Tip:** Pack a picnic and find a spot along the shore to watch the ferry come and go. The comings and goings of the boat are the island's main source of excitement, and locals often gather to greet arriving visitors.

## LESSER-KNOWN GEMS OF CASCO BAY

While Peaks, Great Diamond, and Cliff Island are the most visited, Casco Bay has several lesser-known islands worth exploring. Little Diamond Island is a peaceful retreat with a mix of private homes and vacation rentals, while Long Island boasts sandy beaches and lush forests.

**Fun Fact:** Casco Bay is home to "the Calendar Islands," so named because legend has it there are 365 islands—one for every day of the year. While the actual number is closer to 200, the bay's diverse landscape offers endless opportunities for exploration.

**Insider Tip:** Consider a private charter with Casco Bay Custom Charters to visit some of the smaller, more remote islands that aren't accessible by ferry.

## THE CASCO BAY FERRY EXPERIENCE

The ferry ride to the islands is an experience in itself. As you leave Portland's bustling waterfront behind, the skyline fades into the distance, and the islands come into view, each with its own character.

Onboard, you'll often see locals commuting alongside visitors, giving you a glimpse into daily life in the bay.

---

**Insider Tip:** Sit on the upper deck of the ferry for the best views, and don't forget your camera—Casco Bay's sunsets are spectacular.

---

## From Islands to Lighthouses

The Casco Bay Islands offer a taste of Maine's natural beauty and maritime history, but the allure of the coast doesn't end there. In the next chapter, we'll journey south to Cape Elizabeth, where iconic lighthouses and rugged cliffs define the landscape. Join us for a closer look at one of Maine's most scenic coastal towns in ***Chapter 21: Cape Elizabeth.***

**21**

# CAPE ELIZABETH

## LAND OF LIGHTHOUSES AND LEGENDS

Cape Elizabeth is a town where rugged cliffs meet the open Atlantic, and the past feels as present as the tide. Known for its iconic lighthouses, serene beaches, and quiet natural beauty, it's a place where every vista tells a story. Just a short drive from Portland, Cape Elizabeth is a must-visit destination for anyone who loves coastal charm mixed with historical intrigue.

## PORTLAND HEAD LIGHT: MAINE'S ICONIC BEACON

**Where:** Fort Williams Park, Cape Elizabeth.

Towering over the rocky coastline, Portland Head Light is not only Maine's oldest lighthouse but also one of the most photographed in the world. Commissioned by George Washington and completed in 1791, the lighthouse has stood as a sentinel for over two centuries, guiding mariners safely through the treacherous waters of Casco Bay.

**The Experience:**

A visit to Portland Head Light begins with the approach through Fort Williams Park, a sprawling public space dotted with historic ruins, picnic areas, and walking trails. The lighthouse itself stands atop a rocky bluff, offering breathtaking views of the Atlantic. Inside the adjacent **Museum** (1000 Shore Rd, Cape Elizabeth, ME 04107), housed in the former keeper's quarters, visitors can explore artifacts and stories that bring the lighthouse's history to life.

---

**Fun Fact:** Henry Wadsworth Longfellow, one of America's most celebrated poets, often visited Portland Head Light and was inspired by its dramatic setting. Some say his poem "The Lighthouse" was written with this beacon in mind.

**Insider Tip:** Bring a picnic and settle on the park's grassy lawn or one of its seaside benches. If you visit in the evening, you'll catch the light beam slicing through the twilight—a sight that feels like stepping into a painting.

---

## TWO LIGHTS STATE PARK: A COASTAL HAVEN

**Where:** Cape Elizabeth.

Named for the twin lighthouses perched on its rocky shoreline, Two Lights State Park is a coastal gem. While the lighthouses themselves are privately owned and not open to the public, the surrounding park offers stunning ocean views and a peaceful escape from the hustle and bustle of Portland.

**The Experience:**

The park's network of trails winds through dense pine forests and opens onto rocky outcroppings that drop dramatically into the sea. At low tide, tidal pools come alive with marine creatures, offering a fascinating glimpse into coastal ecology.

**Local Insight:** The twin lighthouses have been immortalized in Edward Hopper's painting "The Lighthouse at Two Lights," which captures their stark beauty against the expansive sky.

**Insider Tip:** Stop by the **Lobster Shack at Two Lights** (225 Two Lights Rd, Cape Elizabeth, ME 04107), a beloved local eatery with picnic tables overlooking the ocean. Their lobster rolls are legendary, and the view makes every bite taste better.

## HIGGINS BEACH: WHERE SURF MEETS HISTORY

**Where:** Ocean Ave, Scarborough, ME 04074.

Higgins Beach is a picturesque strip of shoreline known for its soft sands, gentle surf, and a hauntingly beautiful shipwreck that emerges at low tide. The wreck's skeletal remains, believed to date back to the 19th century, add a touch of mystery to this serene spot.

### The Experience:

Surfers flock to Higgins Beach for its consistent waves, while families enjoy its calm waters and tide pools. The shipwreck, located near the mouth of the Spurwink River, is a favorite for photographers and history enthusiasts alike.

**Fun Fact:** The origins of the wreck remain a mystery, with some locals speculating it was a schooner lost in a storm over a century ago.

**Insider Tip:** Visit early in the morning to catch the sunrise, casting a golden glow over the beach and the shipwreck. If you're a surfer, check local surf reports before heading out to catch the best waves.

## THE ALLURE OF CRESCENT BEACH

**Where:** 109 Bowery Beach Rd, Cape Elizabeth, ME 04107.

Crescent Beach lives up to its name with a mile-long stretch of sand that curves gently along the shoreline. Flanked by rolling dunes and pine forests, the beach is perfect for sunbathing, swimming, and picnicking.

**The Experience:**

The calm waters make Crescent Beach ideal for families, while kayakers and paddleboarders often take to the waves to explore the nearby coastline. In the off-season, the beach becomes a peaceful retreat for walkers and nature lovers.

---

**Insider Tip:** Rent a paddleboard from a local outfitter and explore the coastline from the water. Keep an eye out for seals and seabirds, which are common sights in the area.

---

## FORT WILLIAMS PARK: MORE THAN A LIGHTHOUSE

**Where:** Cape Elizabeth.

While Portland Head Light is the crown jewel of Fort Williams Park, the park itself offers much more to explore. Wander through the ruins of Fort Williams, a former military outpost, or follow the cliffside trails that wind along the coastline.

**The Experience:**

The park's scenic views and wide-open spaces make it a favorite for locals and visitors alike. Seasonal flower gardens add a splash of color, while the Children's Garden offers interactive exhibits that teach kids about local flora and fauna.

**Fun Fact:** Fort Williams was an active military installation from 1899 to 1962 and played a key role in defending Portland Harbor during both World Wars.

**Insider Tip:** Visit in late summer or early fall to see the gardens at their peak and enjoy cooler temperatures for exploring the trails.

## ARTISTIC INSPIRATION IN CAPE ELIZABETH

Cape Elizabeth has long been a muse for artists, from painters like Edward Hopper to contemporary photographers. Its dramatic coastline, iconic lighthouses, and ever-changing light create a palette that has inspired countless works of art.

**Fun Fact:** Many of Hopper's sketches and paintings of Cape Elizabeth are now housed in prestigious galleries, including the Whitney Museum of American Art in New York.

**Insider Tip:** Bring your own sketchbook or camera and see how the landscape inspires you. Some local art studios even offer plein-air painting workshops for visitors.

## EXPLORING FREEPORT'S UNIQUE BLEND

Cape Elizabeth is a place where natural beauty and history converge, but Maine has even more to offer. Just a short drive north, Freeport combines world-class shopping with stunning outdoor adventures. In the next chapter, we'll explore everything from L.L. Bean's flagship store to the trails and dunes of Wolfe's Neck Woods in ***Chapter 22: Freeport.***

# FREEPORT



## WHERE SHOPPING MEETS ADVENTURE

Freeport, just a short 20-minute drive north of Portland, is a place where the thrill of exploration extends beyond nature to bustling shops, local eateries, and cultural attractions. Known as the home of L.L. Bean's flagship store, Freeport surprises visitors with its blend of outdoor adventures, historic charm, and unique attractions like the Desert of Maine. Whether you're an outdoor enthusiast, a dedicated shopper, or a history buff, Freeport offers something for everyone.

## L.L. BEAN: A NEW ENGLAND ICON

**Where:** 95 Main St, Freeport.

L.L. Bean isn't just a store—it's a destination. Founded in 1912 by Leon Leonwood Bean, this world-famous outdoor retailer has been headquartered in Freeport for over a century. The flagship store is open 24 hours a day, 365 days a year, welcoming visitors from around the globe.

**The Experience:**

The store is more than a place to shop for rugged boots and flannel shirts. It features an expansive layout with sections dedicated to camping, fishing, hunting, and more. Beyond shopping, visitors can enjoy free events such as outdoor concerts, seasonal festivals, and hands-on workshops in fly fishing, kayaking, and wilderness skills.

---

**Fun Fact:** Outside the store, you'll find the iconic giant boot, a 16-foot replica of L.L. Bean's first product, the Maine Hunting Shoe. It's a popular photo spot and a symbol of Freeport's connection to outdoor adventure.

**Insider Tip:** Visit during the annual L.L. Bean Summer in the Park concert series, which brings live music and activities to Freeport's bustling downtown.

---

## WOLFE'S NECK WOODS STATE PARK: A NATURAL RETREAT

**Where:** 426 Wolfe's Neck Rd, Freeport, ME 04032.

Just a few miles from Freeport's town center, Wolfe's Neck Woods State Park offers a peaceful escape into nature. With its mix of forested trails, rocky shorelines, and sweeping views of Casco Bay, the park is a favorite for hikers, birdwatchers, and picnickers.

**The Experience:**

The park's five miles of trails range from easy loops to more rugged coastal paths. The Casco Bay Trail is a standout, leading visitors to breathtaking views of the bay and its islands. Osprey nests are a common sight along the shore, and during nesting season, you might spot these majestic birds soaring overhead.

---

**Fun Fact:** Wolfe's Neck Woods State Park is home to one of the largest osprey populations in Maine. Interpretive signs along the trails provide fascinating insights into these birds and their habitat.

**Insider Tip:** Pack a picnic and enjoy it at one of the park's scenic tables overlooking the water. If you're visiting in the fall, the park's vibrant foliage adds a magical touch to the trails.

## THE DESERT OF MAINE: A SURPRISING ODDITY

**Where:** 95 Desert Rd, Freeport, ME 04032.

The Desert of Maine is a natural sand dune nestled in the heart of a forest—a curious geological phenomenon caused by centuries of soil erosion. Once farmland, the area was abandoned in the late 1800s, leaving behind a striking landscape of rolling sand dunes surrounded by lush greenery.

**The Experience:**

Visitors can explore the desert via guided or self-guided tours, learning about its unique history and ecology. The site also features a historic farmhouse museum and nature trails that wind through the surrounding woods. Special events, such as star-gazing nights and eco-workshops, add to the desert's appeal.

**Fun Fact:** Despite its name, the Desert of Maine is not a true desert—it receives ample rainfall but lacks the nutrients to support vegetation.

**Insider Tip:** Visit during the evening for one of the desert's stargazing events. The lack of light pollution creates an ideal setting for spotting constellations and planets.

## DISCOVERING FREEPORT'S LOCAL CHARM

While L.L. Bean and the Desert of Maine are major draws, Freeport's downtown area is a delight for those who love unique shops and local flavors. From artisanal bakeries to cozy bookstores, the town's Main Street offers plenty of opportunities to explore.

**Local Highlights:**

- **Petrillo's Restaurant and Bar** (15 Depot St, Freeport, ME 04032): A family-owned eatery serving fresh pasta and wood-fired pizzas.
- **The Harraseeket Inn** (162 Main St, Freeport, ME 04032): A charming historic inn offering farm-to-table dining at its on-site restaurant, Broad Arrow Tavern.
- **Sherman's Maine Coast Book Shop** (128 Main St, Freeport, ME 04032): A beloved independent bookstore with a wide selection of regional titles and gifts.

---

**Insider Tip:** Take a walk along Freeport's historic district, where 18th- and 19th-century buildings house modern shops and galleries. Many structures have plaques detailing their original use, offering a glimpse into the town's past.

---

## OUTDOOR ADVENTURES BEYOND FREEPORT

Freeport's proximity to the coast and countryside makes it an excellent base for exploring Maine's natural beauty. In addition to Wolfe's Neck Woods, consider visiting:

- **Mast Landing Sanctuary** (1200 Mast Rd, Freeport, ME 04032): A tranquil spot for birdwatching and hiking, located just minutes from downtown Freeport.
- **Winslow Memorial Park** (17 Staples Point Rd, Freeport,

ME 04032): A waterfront park with picnic areas, a playground, and panoramic views of Casco Bay.

## SEASONAL EVENTS IN FREEPORT

Freeport's vibrant community calendar ensures there's always something happening. Highlights include:

- **Fall Festival:** A weekend of live music, art, and local food held every October.
- **Flavors of Freeport:** A winter food festival showcasing the town's best restaurants and culinary talent.
- **Freeport Sparkle Celebration:** A festive holiday event featuring a parade, tree lighting, and holiday market.

---

**Insider Tip:** Check Freeport's visitor website before your trip to see what events coincide with your visit.

---

## SERENITY AT SEBAGO LAKE

Freeport's mix of shopping, nature, and unique attractions makes it a destination you'll want to linger in. But for those seeking even greater tranquility, Sebago Lake offers a peaceful retreat just a short drive inland. In the next chapter, we'll explore the pristine waters, forested shores, and lakeside cabins that make Sebago Lake an unforgettable escape.

**23**

# SEBAGO LAKE

## MAINE'S TRANQUIL RETREAT

If you've ever dreamed of escaping to a serene, picturesque lake surrounded by lush forests and pristine shorelines, Sebago Lake is the place to be. Just a 40-minute drive from Portland, this tranquil destination offers an idyllic escape from city life. From fishing and boating to hiking and relaxing in cozy lakeside cabins, Sebago Lake is where Maine's natural beauty shines brightest.

## SEBAGO LAKE: A NATURAL WONDER

**Where:** 11 Park Access Rd, Casco, ME 04015.

Sebago Lake is Maine's second-largest lake, stretching over 45 square miles with depths exceeding 300 feet, making it one of the cleanest and most scenic freshwater destinations in the region. It's a haven for outdoor enthusiasts, families, and anyone seeking peace and quiet in a breathtaking natural setting.

**The Experience:**

Visitors flock to Sebago Lake for its crystal-clear waters and endless opportunities for adventure. Fishing is a popular activity, with the lake teeming with landlocked salmon, lake trout, and bass. Boating is another favorite pastime—whether you prefer paddleboarding, kayaking, or cruising in a motorboat, Sebago's calm waters offer the perfect playground.

For those who prefer to stay on land, Sebago Lake State Park provides over 1,400 acres of forested trails, sandy beaches, and picnic areas. The park's hiking trails range from easy walks to more challenging routes, each offering stunning views of the lake and its surroundings.

**Fun Fact:** Sebago Lake serves as the primary drinking water source for Portland and its neighboring towns, making it one of the most important natural resources in the state.

**Insider Tip:** Arrive early during the summer months to secure a prime spot on the beach or a rental boat. For a quieter experience, visit in the fall when the foliage transforms the area into a kaleidoscope of reds, oranges, and yellows.

## FISHING AND BOATING AT SEBAGO

Fishing is a year-round activity at Sebago Lake, with each season offering unique opportunities. In the spring and summer, anglers can cast their lines for salmon and lake trout, while winter brings ice-fishing enthusiasts to the frozen expanse of the lake.

Boating is equally popular, and several marinas around the lake offer rentals for kayaks, canoes, and motorboats. Sebago is also home to several small islands, including Frye Island, which features its own beaches, hiking trails, and a charming general store.

**Insider Tip:** Hire a local guide for a fishing excursion. They'll share their insider knowledge of the lake's best fishing spots and techniques, ensuring a successful day on the water.

## LAKEFRONT CABINS AND LODGING

Sebago Lake's shoreline is dotted with charming lakefront cabins, ranging from rustic retreats to luxurious accommodations. These cabins provide the perfect home base for exploring the area or simply unwinding by the water.

Many cabins come equipped with private docks, fire pits, and panoramic views of the lake, making them ideal for families, couples, or solo travelers seeking a peaceful getaway.

**Fun Fact:** Many of the cabins around Sebago are family-owned and have been passed down through generations, adding a sense of history and tradition to your stay.

**Insider Tip:** Book your cabin early, especially during peak summer months or fall foliage season. Properties with private lake access are in high demand and fill up quickly.

## HIKING AND EXPLORING AROUND SEBAGO

The area surrounding Sebago Lake is a hiker's paradise, with trails that wind through forests, wetlands, and along rocky shorelines. Popular trails include:

- **The Bald Pate Mountain Trail:** A moderately challenging hike that rewards visitors with stunning views of Sebago Lake and the surrounding region.
- **The Douglas Mountain Preserve Trail:** A short but steep trail leading to an open summit with panoramic vistas.
- **The Sebago to the Sea Trail:** A multi-use path that

stretches from Sebago Lake all the way to Casco Bay, perfect for biking or long-distance hiking.

---

**Insider Tip:** Bring sturdy shoes and plenty of water, especially for the more challenging trails. During the summer, pack bug spray to keep mosquitoes at bay.

---

## HIDDEN GEMS OF SEBAGO LAKE

While Sebago Lake's beaches and trails are well-known, the area also offers a few hidden treasures for adventurous visitors.

- **Songo River Lock:** This historic hand-operated lock connects Sebago Lake to Long Lake and is a fascinating stop for history buffs. Watching boats navigate the lock is both entertaining and educational.
- **Trickey Pond:** A small, crystal-clear pond near Sebago Lake that's perfect for swimming, paddleboarding, and kayaking. Its quiet atmosphere makes it a favorite among locals.
- **Frye Island:** Accessible by ferry, this island offers a peaceful retreat with quiet beaches, walking trails, and a welcoming community feel.

---

**Insider Tip:** Pack a picnic and take the ferry to Frye Island for a day of exploring its charming nooks and crannies.

---

## SEASONAL HIGHLIGHTS AT SEBAGO LAKE

Sebago Lake offers something special in every season.

- **Summer:** Enjoy warm days on the beach, boating, and outdoor dining at local lakefront restaurants.

- **Fall:** The foliage around Sebago is nothing short of spectacular. Take a drive along the lake's edge or hike to a summit for the best views.
- **Winter:** Ice fishing, snowshoeing, and cross-country skiing transform the lake into a winter wonderland.
- **Spring:** The snowmelt swells the lake's rivers and streams, creating perfect conditions for kayaking and fly fishing.

**Insider Tip:** Visit in late September or early October for peak foliage combined with fewer crowds. The crisp air and vibrant colors make this the most magical time to experience Sebago.

## LOCAL DINING AND CULTURE

While Sebago Lake is known for its natural beauty, it also boasts a handful of excellent dining options. Lakeside restaurants like **The Galley Restaurant & Pub** (327 Roosevelt Trail, Naples, ME 04055) and **Rick's Café** (286 Roosevelt Trail, Naples, ME 04055) serve fresh seafood and local fare, often with outdoor seating that offers views of the water.

For a taste of local culture, check out the Sebago Days Festival in July, a community celebration featuring live music, carnival games, and food trucks.

**Insider Tip:** End your day with a classic Maine treat: a blueberry pie or a lobster roll from one of the local eateries.

## EXPANDING YOUR HORIZONS

Sebago Lake offers the perfect mix of relaxation and adventure, but there's even more to explore beyond the Portland area. From the colonial charm of Portsmouth, New Hampshire, to the rugged beauty of Bar Harbor and Acadia National Park, Maine's day trip destinations are as diverse as they are captivating. Join us in Chapter 24 as we journey south to Portsmouth, where history meets modern-day vibrancy.

24

# PORTSMOUTH, NEW HAMPSHIRE

## WHERE HISTORY MEETS MODERN VIBRANCY

An hour south of Portland, across the Piscataqua River, lies Portsmouth, New Hampshire—a coastal town that feels like a step back in time with a contemporary twist. With cobblestone streets, colonial architecture, and a thriving arts and culinary scene, Portsmouth is a perfect blend of New England charm and urban sophistication. Whether you're strolling through historic neighborhoods, dining at award-winning restaurants, or exploring its bustling harbor, Portsmouth offers an unforgettable day trip packed with stories and surprises.

## MARKET SQUARE: THE HEART OF PORTSMOUTH

**Where:** 1 Market St, Portsmouth, NH 03801.

Market Square is the beating heart of Portsmouth, a bustling hub where past and present collide. Lined with charming brick buildings, unique shops, art galleries, and cozy cafés, it's the perfect place to start your exploration.

**The Experience:**

Begin your visit with a leisurely stroll around the square, where you'll find everything from boutique stores offering local crafts to bookshops brimming with rare finds. For art enthusiasts, galleries like **Discover Portsmouth** showcase the work of local and regional artists, while live music performances often fill the air with energy.

---

**Fun Fact:** Market Square was once home to Portsmouth's first town hall and has served as the epicenter of commerce since the 17th century.

**Insider Tip:** Stop by **Ceres Bakery** (51 Penhallow St, Portsmouth, NH 03801) for a pastry or coffee before exploring the side streets radiating from the square—they're filled with hidden gems, including specialty shops and quiet courtyards.

---

## STRAWBERY BANKE MUSEUM: A LIVING TIME CAPSULE

**Where:** 14 Hancock St, Portsmouth, NH 03801.

Strawbery Banke Museum is a must-visit for history buffs. This 10-acre living history museum recreates life in Portsmouth from the 17th through the 20th centuries, with restored homes, gardens, and costumed interpreters bringing history to life.

**The Experience:**

As you wander through the museum's grounds, you'll step into homes representing different eras, from colonial taverns to Victorian parlors. Interact with costumed reenactors who share stories of daily life, historic events, and Portsmouth's role in America's maritime history. Seasonal events, such as the **Candlelight Stroll** during the holidays, add a magical touch.

**Fun Fact:** The museum gets its name from the original settlement of Strawbery Banke, established in 1630 along the Piscataqua River.

**Insider Tip:** Visit during spring or summer to see the heritage gardens in full bloom, or plan your trip around a special event like the Fall Festival or the holiday Candlelight Stroll.

## PRESCOTT PARK: A RIVERSIDE OASIS

**Where:** 14 Hancock St, Portsmouth, NH 03801.

Prescott Park is a serene escape on the waterfront, offering beautifully landscaped gardens, walking paths, and stunning views of the Piscataqua River. It's a perfect spot for a picnic or a moment of quiet reflection.

### The Experience:

The park's flowerbeds burst with color in the spring and summer, while its open-air pavilion hosts live performances, including the popular **Prescott Park Arts Festival.** Visitors can also watch boats sail by or take a short walk to the nearby fishing pier.

**Fun Fact:** Prescott Park was established in the 1930s after sisters Josie and Mary Prescott donated the land to the city to preserve the waterfront for public use.

**Insider Tip:** Check the schedule for the Prescott Park Arts Festival, which includes outdoor concerts, theatrical performances, and movie nights under the stars.

## PORTSMOUTH'S CULINARY SCENE

Portsmouth's food scene rivals that of much larger cities, offering everything from fresh seafood to inventive farm-to-table creations.

- **The Black Trumpet Bistro** (105 Marcy St, Portsmouth, NH 03801): A two-story eatery in a historic building specializing in globally inspired dishes made with local ingredients.
- **Portsmouth Brewery** (56 Market St, Portsmouth, NH 03801): The oldest craft brewery in New Hampshire, serving house-made beers and pub fare in a lively atmosphere.
- **Row 34** (5 Portwalk Pl, Portsmouth, NH 03801): Known for its exceptional oyster bar and fresh seafood, it's a must-visit for seafood lovers.

---

**Fun Fact:** Portsmouth has more restaurants per capita than most U.S. cities, making it a culinary hotspot.

**Insider Tip:** For dessert, head to **Annabelle's Natural Ice Cream** for a scoop of their homemade treats, with flavors ranging from classic vanilla to maple walnut.

---

## PORTSMOUTH HARBOR LIGHTHOUSE: A MARITIME TREASURE

**Where:** 25 Wentworth Rd, New Castle, NH 03854.

Located at Fort Constitution, the Portsmouth Harbor Lighthouse has guided ships into the Piscataqua River since 1771. While the current lighthouse dates to 1878, its history stretches back to the Revolutionary War.

**The Experience:**

Visitors can climb to the top of the lighthouse on select days for panoramic views of the river, the harbor, and the ocean beyond. The tour also includes a fascinating look at the lighthouse's inner workings and its historical significance.

---

**Fun Fact:** The lighthouse is rumored to be haunted by the ghost of a former keeper who reportedly whistles on stormy nights.

**Insider Tip:** Tours are seasonal and fill up quickly, so book your spot in advance through the **Friends of Portsmouth Harbor Lighthouses** website.

---

## SEASONAL HIGHLIGHTS IN PORTSMOUTH

Portsmouth's charm shifts with the seasons, offering unique experiences year-round.

- **Summer:** Enjoy the Prescott Park Arts Festival, harbor cruises, and outdoor dining.
- **Fall:** Take a scenic drive through the foliage or visit during the Halloween Parade, a quirky local tradition.
- **Winter:** Stroll through Strawbery Banke's Candlelight Stroll and enjoy festive decorations throughout downtown.
- **Spring:** Wander the town's gardens and parks as the flowers bloom.

---

**Insider Tip:** Portsmouth's coastal location means the weather is often milder than inland New Hampshire, making it an ideal destination even in cooler months.

---

## PORTSMOUTH HARBOR CRUISES AND RIVERWALK

To truly appreciate Portsmouth's maritime heritage, take a harbor cruise or explore the city's Riverwalk. Cruises offer guided tours of the harbor's lighthouses, forts, and islands, while the Riverwalk connects downtown Portsmouth to picturesque views of the Piscataqua.

---

**Insider Tip:** Sunset cruises are particularly magical, as the fading light casts a golden glow over the water and the town.

---

## The Rugged Beauty of Bar Harbor

Portsmouth's blend of history, charm, and modern energy makes it a perfect day trip destination. But if you're craving a grander adventure, Bar Harbor and Acadia National Park await. In the next chapter, we'll explore this iconic Maine destination, where towering cliffs, breathtaking vistas, and charming small-town vibes promise an unforgettable experience.

## 25

# BAR HARBOR AND ACADIA NATIONAL PARK

## A JOURNEY TO MAINE'S CROWN JEWEL

If Portland is Maine's bustling heart, Bar Harbor and Acadia National Park are its wild, untamed soul. Located about two and a half hours north of Portland, Bar Harbor is a charming coastal town brimming with boutiques, art galleries, and fresh seafood, all set against the dramatic backdrop of Acadia National Park. This is where granite cliffs meet crashing waves, and forested trails lead to panoramic vistas. Whether you're an outdoor adventurer, a history enthusiast, or a lover of small-town charm, Bar Harbor is worth every mile of the journey.

## ACADIA NATIONAL PARK: NATURE'S MASTERPIECE

**Where:** Headquarters: 25 Visitor Center Rd, Bar Harbor, ME 04609.

Spanning more than 49,000 acres, Acadia National Park is one of the most visited national parks in the United States. Its rugged coastline, lush forests, and granite peaks create a landscape that's both majestic and serene. The park is a haven for hikers, cyclists, and nature lovers, offering endless opportunities to connect with Maine's raw beauty.

**The Experience:**

Start your visit with a drive along the **Park Loop Road**, a 27-mile scenic route that winds through the park's most iconic sites. Along the way, stop at **Sand Beach** (Park Loop Rd, Bar Harbor, ME 04609), a stunning crescent of sand framed by rocky cliffs, and **Thunder Hole** (Park Loop Rd, Bar Harbor, ME 04609), a natural rock formation where waves crash with a thunderous roar.

For hikers, the **Precipice Trail** offers a challenging ascent with iron rungs and ladders, while the more accessible **Jordan Pond Path** (2928 Park Loop Rd, Seal Harbor, ME 04675) provides serene views of the park's crystal-clear waters and the iconic Bubbles Mountains.

---

**A Personal Touch:** At sunrise on Cadillac Mountain, the highest point on the U.S. East Coast, Channa and Stephen got engaged. As the first rays of light touched the horizon, their moment was as breathtaking as the panoramic views stretching across the Atlantic.

**Fun Fact:** Cadillac Mountain is one of the first places in the U.S. to see the sunrise. It's a magical experience that draws early risers from around the world.

**Insider Tip:** Arrive early to avoid crowds, especially during peak summer months. If you're planning to watch the sunrise from Cadillac Mountain, secure a reservation online—it's a popular experience that fills up quickly.

---

## BAR HARBOR: COASTAL CHARM MEETS ADVENTURE

**Where:** Town Center: 93 Cottage St, Bar Harbor, ME 04609.

Bar Harbor is more than just a gateway to Acadia—it's a destination in its own right. The town's streets are lined with quaint shops, vibrant galleries, and inviting restaurants, all exuding a warm, small-town vibe.

**The Experience:**

Spend the morning browsing local boutiques like **Window Panes** (166 Main St, Bar Harbor, ME 04609) for home goods or **Island Artisans** (99 Main St, Bar Harbor, ME 04609) for handcrafted jewelry and gifts. Stroll along the **Shore Path** (begins at 1 Newport Dr, Bar Harbor, ME 04609), a peaceful coastal walk that offers breathtaking views of Frenchman Bay and the Porcupine Islands.

For lunch, stop at **Stewman's Lobster Pound** (35 West St, Bar Harbor, ME 04609), where you can enjoy fresh lobster while sitting dockside. In the afternoon, hop aboard a **whale-watching tour** with Bar Harbor Whale Watch Co. (1 West St, Bar Harbor, ME 04609) or a **schooner cruise** departing from the town pier.

---

**Fun Fact:** Bar Harbor was a summer retreat for America's wealthiest families during the Gilded Age, and many of their grand mansions still stand today.

**Insider Tip:** Visit the Bar Harbor Historical Society (33 Ledgelawn Ave, Bar Harbor, ME 04609) to learn about the town's rich past, including its transformation from a Gilded Age resort to a modern tourist hub.

---

## JORDAN POND: A DINING AND SCENIC HIGHLIGHT

**Where:** 2928 Park Loop Rd, Seal Harbor, ME 04675.

Jordan Pond is one of the most picturesque spots in Acadia, with its calm waters reflecting the surrounding mountains. Adjacent to the pond is the **Jordan Pond House**, a historic restaurant famous for its popovers and tea.

**The Experience:**

After a hike along the Jordan Pond Path, reward yourself with a meal at the Jordan Pond House. Sit on the lawn patio for the best views while you enjoy their signature popovers, served warm with butter and jam.

---

**Fun Fact:** The Jordan Pond House has been a tradition in Acadia since the late 19th century, making it as much a part of the park's history as its trails.

**Insider Tip:** Arrive early or make a reservation to avoid long waits, especially during peak dining hours.

---

## SEASONAL HIGHLIGHTS IN BAR HARBOR AND ACADIA

Bar Harbor and Acadia National Park offer unique experiences in every season.

- **Summer:** Ideal for hiking, whale watching, and kayaking along the rugged coastline.
- **Fall:** Acadia's foliage transforms the park into a vivid tapestry of red, orange, and yellow. The crisp air is perfect for outdoor exploration.
- **Winter:** Snowshoeing and cross-country skiing provide a peaceful way to enjoy the park's quieter season.
- **Spring:** Wildflowers bloom, and the park comes alive with birdsong and flowing streams from the snowmelt.

---

**Insider Tip:** Visit in late September or early October for peak foliage and fewer crowds.

---

## THE GILDED AGE MANSIONS OF BAR HARBOR

During the late 19th century, Bar Harbor was a summer retreat for America's elite, including families like the Rockefellers, Morgans, and Astors. While many of the grand "cottages" were lost to the Great Fire of 1947, a few still remain, offering a glimpse into the town's glamorous past.

**Must-See Mansion:** La Rochelle Mansion and Museum (127 West St, Bar Harbor, ME 04609) provides guided tours that explore the architecture and lifestyle of Bar Harbor's Gilded Age residents.

---

**Insider Tip:** Take a guided walking tour of West Street to see the remaining mansions and learn about their fascinating histories.

---

## OUTDOOR ADVENTURES BEYOND ACADIA

While Acadia dominates the landscape, there are other outdoor activities around Bar Harbor worth exploring.

- **Schoodic Peninsula:** A quieter section of Acadia National Park offering dramatic coastline views and fewer crowds.
- **Isle au Haut:** Accessible by ferry, this remote island offers pristine hiking trails and a glimpse into traditional island life.
- **Frenchman Bay:** Rent a kayak and paddle through the bay, exploring its coves and spotting wildlife like seals and bald eagles.

---

**Insider Tip:** For a truly unique experience, book a bioluminescent night paddle tour in Frenchman Bay to see the water glow with natural light.

---

## DINING AND NIGHTLIFE IN BAR HARBOR

Bar Harbor's dining scene is a feast for the senses, with fresh seafood and innovative dishes taking center stage.

- **Café This Way:** 14 Mount Desert St, Bar Harbor, ME 04609.
- **Side Street Café:** 49 Rodick St, Bar Harbor, ME 04609.
- **Thrive Juice Bar and Kitchen:** 65 Main St, Bar Harbor, ME 04609.

For nightlife, head to **The Lompoc Café** (36 Rodick St, Bar Harbor, ME 04609) for live music or enjoy a drink at **Bar Harbor Beerworks** (119 Main St, Bar Harbor, ME 04609), a lively spot with an extensive beer list.

---

**Insider Tip:** End your evening with a stroll along the Shore Path under the stars. The town's minimal light pollution makes it an excellent place for stargazing.

---

## A Return to Portland's Charm

Bar Harbor and Acadia National Park are the perfect culmination of any Maine adventure, offering breathtaking landscapes and unforgettable experiences. But as your day trip comes to a close, Portland awaits with its own brand of charm and warmth. Whether you're heading back to enjoy the city or planning your next excursion, Portland is always ready to welcome you home.

# PART 5: PLANNING YOUR TRIP TO PORTLAND, MAINE

**26**

# WHERE TO STAY

## REST EASY IN PORTLAND

Portland's diverse accommodations are as vibrant and unique as the city itself. Whether you're dreaming of waking up to the sound of waves on a houseboat, staying in a historic mansion, or finding the perfect place to bring your furry friend, Portland offers something for every traveler. This chapter explores the city's most intriguing lodging options and provides tips to match every type of traveler with the ideal stay.

## HOTELS, INNS, AND VACATION RENTALS FOR ALL BUDGETS

### _Luxury Stays: A Touch of Elegance_

**The Press Hotel**

- **Where:** 119 Exchange St, Portland, ME 04101.
- **Website:** www.thepresshotel.com.

Located in the historic _Portland Press Herald_ building, this boutique hotel seamlessly blends nostalgia with modern design. Each room reflects Portland's creative spirit, featuring typewriter-inspired décor and sleek furnishings.

---

**Insider Tip:** Request a room on the upper floors for the best city views.

---

## Cove Island Lodge

- **Where:** 145 Cove St, Portland, ME 04101.

Nestled on a small private island, this hidden gem offers a truly tranquil retreat just minutes from the city center. Accessible only by boat, the lodge combines seclusion with luxury, offering private docks and waterfront views.

---

**Fun Fact:** The lodge's dockside dining menu is sourced entirely from local Maine farms and fisheries.

**Insider Tip:** Perfect for couples seeking romance or writers looking for inspiration.

---

### *Mid-Range Options: Comfort Meets Convenience*

## Inn at St. John

- **Where:** 939 Congress St, Portland, ME 04102.
- **Website:** www.innatstjohn.com.

A historic gem dating back to 1897, this inn charms guests with its antique furnishings, cozy atmosphere, and budget-friendly rates.

**Insider Tip:** Ask the staff about the inn's fascinating past—it's the oldest continuously operating lodging in Portland.

## Blind Tiger Guesthouse

- **Where:** 163 Danforth St, Portland, ME 04102.
- **Website:** www.blindtigerportland.com.

This 19th-century mansion combines boutique luxury with a modern twist. The house is filled with curated art and playful details, like billiards in the lounge.

**Fun Fact:** The guesthouse is named after a Prohibition-era term for speakeasies.

**Insider Tip:** Enjoy complimentary wine and snacks in the evenings—a guesthouse tradition.

### *Budget-Friendly Gems: Affordable and Inviting*

## The Black Elephant Hostel

- **Where:** 33 Hampshire St, Portland, ME 04101.
- **Website:** www.blackelephantinn.com.

This hostel feels like a community hub, offering dorm and private rooms in a colorful, artsy space.

**Insider Tip:** Check out the events board in the common area for local happenings—often, staff post insider recommendations.

## Hi-Portland Hostel (Eastern Promenade)

- **Where:** 65 India St, Portland, ME 04101.
- **Website:** www.hiusa.org.

Perfectly situated near the Eastern Promenade, this hostel offers affordable accommodations with million-dollar views of Casco Bay.

## UNIQUE STAYS: WATERFRONT RETREATS AND HISTORIC CHARM

### Stay on a Houseboat

- **Where:** DiMillo's Marina, 1 Long Wharf, Portland, ME 04101.
- **Website:** Search for houseboat listings on Airbnb.

For a truly one-of-a-kind experience, stay on a houseboat docked in Portland's harbor. These floating retreats provide cozy quarters and unmatched views of the waterfront. Fall asleep to the gentle sway of the boat and wake up to seabirds and harbor activity.

---

**Insider Tip:** Pack light—space is limited—but don't forget a camera for sunrise over Casco Bay.

---

### Overnight on a Yacht

- **Where:** Available at various Portland marinas.

For luxury travelers, booking an overnight stay on a privately chartered yacht combines the elegance of a five-star hotel with the exclusivity of a waterfront view. Companies like **Yacht Getaways Maine** offer curated stays with on-board meals and sunset sails.

---

**Fun Fact:** Many yachts in Portland harbor double as chartered dining experiences during the day, transforming into private stays at night.

---

## PET-FRIENDLY ACCOMMODATIONS

### The Francis

- **Where:** 747 Congress St, Portland, ME 04102.
- **Website:** www.thefrancismaine.com.

This boutique property ensures pets are pampered alongside their owners. With pet-friendly suites, welcome treats, and nearby parks, it's perfect for travelers with furry companions.

### Inn by the Sea

- **Where:** 40 Bowery Beach Rd, Cape Elizabeth, ME 04107.
- **Website:** www.innbythesea.com.

A short drive from Portland, this luxurious property goes above and beyond for pets, offering gourmet dog menus, beach walks, and even pet massage services.

---

**Insider Tip:** Take advantage of their "Beach Package," which includes pet-friendly amenities and access to Crescent Beach.

---

## TIPS FOR DIFFERENT TRAVELERS

### Families

- Look for accommodations with kitchenettes, like **Residence Inn by Marriott Downtown/Waterfront** (145 Fore St,

Portland, ME 04101). Having access to a kitchen makes traveling with kids much more manageable.

- Choose hotels near parks like Deering Oaks or the Eastern Promenade for outdoor play.

## Couples

- Opt for romantic inns like **The Chadwick Bed & Breakfast** or waterfront escapes like a houseboat stay.
- Consider booking a room at **The Press Hotel**, known for its sophisticated ambiance and luxurious touches.

## Solo Travelers

- Budget-friendly options like **The Black Elephant Hostel** offer opportunities to meet fellow travelers while maintaining privacy in private rooms.
- Stay near the Old Port district to maximize access to dining, shopping, and nightlife.

## Luxury Seekers

- Splurge on the **Portland Harbor Hotel** or a private yacht stay for an unforgettable experience.
- Seek out high-end vacation rentals through **Docent's Collection**, offering impeccable service and stunning décor.

## Outdoor Enthusiasts

- Stay near the Eastern Promenade for quick access to walking trails and kayaking.
- Look for properties with bike rentals or storage for outdoor gear.

## Savoring Portland's Cuisine

Now that you've discovered the perfect place to stay, it's time to experience the city's culinary magic. From lobster rolls by the water to late-night snacks in cozy pubs, Chapter 27 will guide you through Portland's legendary food and drink scene. Prepare your taste buds for adventure!

# 27

# WHERE TO EAT AND DRINK IN PORTLAND, MAINE

## A CITY THAT EATS LIKE A NATION

In Portland, food is more than sustenance—it's a way of life. Every street and waterfront corner hides a culinary masterpiece waiting to be discovered, from fresh-caught lobster rolls to meticulously crafted international cuisine. Here, James Beard Award winners rub elbows with hidden gems only locals know about. Portland's dining scene reflects the city itself: welcoming, innovative, and brimming with character. Whether you're chasing a perfect croissant, a frothy IPA, or a dinner worthy of a celebration, Portland offers a taste for every traveler. This chapter is your guide to experiencing the city one delicious bite at a time.

## SEAFOOD: THE HEARTBEAT OF PORTLAND'S CUISINE

Portland's seafood scene is legendary, offering some of the freshest flavors the Atlantic has to offer. From buttery lobster rolls to briny oysters and steaming bowls of clam chowder, the city is a haven for seafood lovers. Here's a curated selection of must-visit seafood spots, each with its own unique story and flavor.

## *Eventide Oyster Co.*

- **Cuisine:** Seafood, Oysters
- **Neighborhood:** Old Port
- **Budget:** $$$
- **Address:** 86 Middle St, Portland, ME 04101
- **Contact:** (207) 774-8538 | eventideoysterco.com

**Their Story:** A James Beard Award-winning restaurant known for its inventive oyster bar and innovative seafood dishes like the brown butter lobster roll.

---

**Insider Tip:** Don't skip their house-made pickles—they pair surprisingly well with the oysters.

**Fun Fact:** The name "Eventide" refers to the evening tide, celebrating the restaurant's deep connection to the sea.

---

## *DiMillo's on the Water*

- **Cuisine:** Seafood, American
- **Neighborhood:** Waterfront
- **Budget:** $$$
- **Address:** 25 Long Wharf, Portland, ME 04101
- **Contact:** (207) 772-2216 | dimillos.com

**Their Story:** A floating restaurant housed in a converted ferry, DiMillo's offers stunning harbor views alongside a menu brimming with fresh seafood.

---

**Insider Tip:** Visit during sunset for an unforgettable dining experience on the water.

**Fun Fact:** The ferry-turned-restaurant is the only one of its kind in Maine.

---

## *Highroller Lobster Co.*

- **Cuisine:** Seafood
- **Neighborhood:** Old Port
- **Budget:** $$
- **Address:** 104 Exchange St, Portland, ME 04101
- **Contact:** (207) 536-1623 | highrollerlobster.com

**Their Story:** From food truck beginnings to a brick-and-mortar hotspot, Highroller Lobster Co. offers creative takes on lobster classics, including lobster tacos and grilled cheese.

---

**Insider Tip:** Ask for their tangy lime mayo—it adds a zesty twist to their lobster roll.

**Fun Fact:** Highroller's team is known for pushing the boundaries of traditional seafood dishes, leading to creations like lobster-topped nachos.

---

## *Luke's Lobster Portland Pier*

- **Cuisine:** Seafood
- **Neighborhood:** Old Port
- **Budget:** $$
- **Address:** 60 Portland Pier, Portland, ME 04101
- **Contact:** (207) 274-6097 | lukeslobster.com

**Their Story:** A local favorite for its direct-from-the-dock lobster and laid-back coastal vibe, Luke's celebrates Maine's fishing heritage.

**Insider Tip:** Try their lobster bisque—it's rich, creamy, and packed with flavor.

**Fun Fact:** Luke's Lobster partners directly with local fishermen to ensure the freshest catch.

## *Gilbert's Chowder House*

- **Cuisine:** Seafood, American
- **Neighborhood:** Old Port
- **Budget:** $
- **Address:** 92 Commercial St, Portland, ME 04101
- **Contact:** (207) 871-5636 | gilbertschowderhouse.com

**Their Story:** A no-frills institution serving up steaming bowls of chowder and classic fried seafood since 1973.

**Insider Tip:** Order the "Fisherman's Platter" for a little bit of everything—perfect for sharing.

**Fun Fact:** Gilbert's clam chowder has won multiple awards, solidifying its place in Portland's seafood lore.

## *The Lobster Shack at Two Lights*

- **Cuisine:** Seafood
- **Neighborhood:** Cape Elizabeth
- **Budget:** $$
- **Address:** 225 Two Lights Rd, Cape Elizabeth, ME 04107
- **Contact:** (207) 799-1677 | lobstershacktwolights.com

**Their Story:** A scenic seafood shack perched on the rocky coast, offering unparalleled ocean views with every bite.

**Insider Tip:** Pair your lobster roll with their famous blueberry pie for the quintessential Maine meal.

**Fun Fact:** This spot has been a local favorite for over 50 years, often featured in travel magazines.

## *Harraseeket Lunch & Lobster*

- **Cuisine:** Seafood
- **Neighborhood:** Freeport
- **Budget:** $$
- **Address:** 36 Main St, South Freeport, ME 04078
- **Contact:** (207) 865-4888 | harraseeketlobster.com

**Their Story:** A quintessential Maine seafood shack located right on the water, Harraseeket offers freshly caught lobster, clams, and haddock.

**Insider Tip:** The lobster stew is a standout—rich, creamy, and loaded with fresh lobster meat.

**Fun Fact:** The shack's outdoor seating provides perfect views of Freeport Harbor.

## AMERICAN: A TASTE OF NEW ENGLAND AND BEYOND

American cuisine in Portland is as diverse as the city itself, offering everything from comforting diners to sophisticated New American fare. This section highlights spots where hearty meals and innovative dishes take center stage, showcasing Maine's rich culinary heritage with a contemporary twist.

### *Becky's Diner*

- **Cuisine:** American, Diner Classics
- **Neighborhood:** Waterfront
- **Budget:** $
- **Address:** 390 Commercial St, Portland, ME 04101
- **Contact:** (207) 773-7070 | beckysdiner.com

**Their Story:** A Portland icon since 1991, Becky's Diner serves hearty breakfasts and comforting diner fare right by the waterfront.

---

**Insider Tip:** Go early to snag a seat and try the fisherman's breakfast special.

**Fun Fact:** Becky's opens before dawn to cater to the city's early-rising fishermen.

---

## The Great Lost Bear

- **Cuisine:** American, Pub Fare
- **Neighborhood:** Woodfords Corner
- **Budget:** $$
- **Address:** 540 Forest Ave, Portland, ME 04101
- **Contact:** (207) 772-0300 | greatlostbear.com

**Their Story:** A quirky, eclectic spot offering an extensive menu of comfort food favorites alongside a staggering list of Maine craft beers.

---

**Insider Tip:** Order the nachos with pulled pork—they're piled high and perfect for sharing.

**Fun Fact:** The Great Lost Bear has over 80 beers on tap, making it a haven for beer enthusiasts.

---

## Congress Bar & Grill

- **Cuisine:** American, Grill
- **Neighborhood:** Downtown
- **Budget:** $
- **Address:** 617 Congress St, Portland, ME 04101
- **Contact:** (207) 828-9944

**Their Story:** This cozy, laid-back grill has been a downtown staple for years, serving simple yet satisfying burgers, sandwiches, and salads.

---

**Insider Tip:** The blackened chicken sandwich is a crowd-pleaser and pairs perfectly with their house-made fries.

**Fun Fact:** The bar features a rotating selection of local craft beers, making it a favorite spot for casual evenings.

---

## *Back Bay Grill*

- **Cuisine:** New American, Fine Dining
- **Neighborhood:** Back Cove
- **Budget:** $$$$
- **Address:** 65 Portland St, Portland, ME 04101
- **Contact:** (207) 772-8833 | backbaygrill.com

**Their Story:** A long-standing Portland institution, Back Bay Grill is known for its elegant yet approachable New American cuisine crafted with seasonal ingredients.

---

**Insider Tip:** The chef's tasting menu is a must-try for those looking to sample the best of what the restaurant offers.

**Fun Fact:** Back Bay Grill's intimate atmosphere makes it a popular choice for anniversaries and special occasions.

---

## CRAFT BEER AND BREWERIES: A HOPPY HAVEN

Portland is synonymous with craft beer, boasting some of the finest breweries in the country. These spots don't just serve beer—they're hubs of creativity and local pride, offering unique brews that reflect Maine's character. Here are the city's best breweries and brewpubs, where every pint tells a story.

### *Allagash Brewing Company*

- **Cuisine:** Craft Beer
- **Neighborhood:** East Deering
- **Budget:** $$
- **Address:** 50 Industrial Way, Portland, ME 04103
- **Contact:** (207) 878-5385 | allagash.com

**Their Story:** A pioneer in the American craft beer scene, Allagash Brewing is best known for its Belgian-inspired brews, especially the iconic Allagash White.

---

**Insider Tip:** Join a brewery tour to learn about their unique brewing process and sample exclusive small-batch beers.

**Fun Fact:** Allagash is a sustainability leader, donating 1% of its profits to environmental causes.

---

### *Bissell Brothers Brewing*

- **Cuisine:** Craft Beer
- **Neighborhood:** Thompson's Point
- **Budget:** $$
- **Address:** 38 Resurgam Pl, Portland, ME 04102
- **Contact:** (207) 808-8258 | bissellbrothers.com

**Their Story:** Founded by two brothers with a love for hops, Bissell Brothers is a favorite among beer enthusiasts, offering creative, hop-forward beers in a vibrant setting.

---

**Insider Tip:** Their flagship beer, Substance Ale, is a must-try and often sells out quickly.

**Fun Fact:** The brewery's name pays homage to the siblings' strong bond and collaborative spirit.

---

## Foundation Brewing Company

- **Cuisine:** Craft Beer
- **Neighborhood:** Industrial Way
- **Budget:** $$
- **Address:** 1 Industrial Way #5, Portland, ME 04103
- **Contact:** (207) 370-8187 | foundationbrew.com

**Their Story:** Known for its experimental approach to brewing, Foundation creates unique beers that push the boundaries of traditional styles.

---

**Insider Tip:** Try Epiphany, their highly acclaimed IPA with a perfect balance of bitterness and tropical notes.

**Fun Fact:** Foundation shares its space with other breweries, creating a one-stop destination for beer lovers.

---

## Rising Tide Brewing Company

- **Cuisine:** Craft Beer
- **Neighborhood:** East Bayside

- **Budget:** $$
- **Address:** 103 Fox St, Portland, ME 04101
- **Contact:** (207) 370-2337 | risingtidebrewing.com

**Their Story:** A family-owned brewery, Rising Tide crafts beers that celebrate Maine's coastal heritage with names inspired by local landmarks and maritime history.

---

**Insider Tip:** Their Maine Island Trail Ale is a refreshing summer favorite and supports environmental conservation efforts.

**Fun Fact:** The brewery often hosts food trucks, live music, and community events.

---

### *Oxbow Blending & Bottling*

- **Cuisine:** Craft Beer
- **Neighborhood:** East Bayside
- **Budget:** $$
- **Address:** 49 Washington Ave, Portland, ME 04101
- **Contact:** (207) 350-0025 | oxbowbeer.com

**Their Story:** Specializing in farmhouse ales and barrel-aged beers, Oxbow brings a rustic charm to Portland's beer scene.

---

**Insider Tip:** Visit during the fall to try their seasonal pumpkin ale—it's like autumn in a glass.

**Fun Fact:** The brewery's name, "Oxbow," refers to the curves of Maine's rivers, symbolizing the fluidity of their brewing style.

---

### *Liquid Riot Bottling Co.*

- **Cuisine:** Brewery, Gastropub
- **Neighborhood:** Old Port
- **Budget:** $$
- **Address:** 250 Commercial St, Portland, ME 04101
- **Contact:** (207) 221-8889 | liquidriot.com

**Their Story:** A unique combination of brewery, distillery, and gastropub, Liquid Riot offers everything from house-made beers to innovative spirits.

**Insider Tip:** Pair their signature cocktails with their small-batch beer flights for a well-rounded experience.

**Fun Fact:** The name "Liquid Riot" is a nod to Portland's historic Prohibition-era riots.

## *Belleflower Brewing Company*

- **Cuisine:** Craft Beer
- **Neighborhood:** East Bayside
- **Budget:** $$
- **Address:** 66 Cove St, Portland, ME 04101
- **Contact:** (207) 613-9070 | belleflowerbeer.com

**Their Story:** This small-batch brewery specializes in innovative beers that highlight local ingredients and community collaboration.

**Insider Tip:** Their seasonal IPAs are a hit—check what's fresh on tap during your visit.

**Fun Fact:** The brewery was started by two childhood friends who turned their homebrewing passion into a thriving business.

### *Stroudwater Distillery*

- **Cuisine:** Brewery, Distillery
- **Neighborhood:** Thompson's Point
- **Budget:** $$
- **Address:** 4 Thompson's Point, Portland, ME 04102
- **Contact:** (207) 536-7811 | stroudwaterdistillery.com

**Their Story:** While known for its house-made spirits, Stroudwater also offers a curated selection of craft beers, blending the best of both worlds.

---

**Insider Tip:** Try their signature whiskey cocktail alongside a beer flight for the ultimate pairing experience.

**Fun Fact:** The distillery is housed in a historic brick building with stunning views of the Fore River.

---

## BAKERIES AND DESSERTS: SWEET TREATS AND BAKED PERFECTION

Portland's bakeries and dessert spots are as diverse as its cuisine, offering everything from donuts and artisanal bread to creamy gelato and handmade ice cream. These cozy establishments blend local flavors with global techniques, ensuring there's always a treat to satisfy your sweet tooth.

### *The Holy Donut*

- **Cuisine:** Donuts
- **Neighborhood:** Old Port
- **Budget:** $
- **Address:** 7 Exchange St, Portland, ME 04101
- **Contact:** (207) 775-7776 | theholydonut.com

**Their Story:** Known for their uniquely Maine potato donuts, The Holy Donut offers a rotating selection of flavors, from classic maple glaze to chocolate sea salt.

---

**Insider Tip:** Arrive early—the most popular flavors sell out quickly!

**Fun Fact:** Each donut contains real mashed potatoes, giving them a dense yet fluffy texture.

---

## *Mount Desert Island Ice Cream*

- **Cuisine:** Ice Cream
- **Neighborhood:** Old Port
- **Budget:** $
- **Address:** 51 Exchange St, Portland, ME 04101
- **Contact:** (207) 699-4314 | mdiic.com

**Their Story:** A small-batch ice cream shop specializing in inventive flavors like sea salt caramel and Maine blueberry.

---

**Insider Tip:** Try their seasonal specials for one-of-a-kind flavors you won't find anywhere else.

**Fun Fact:** Former President Barack Obama once enjoyed a cone from Mount Desert Island Ice Cream during a Maine visit.

---

## *Belleville Bakery*

- **Cuisine:** French Bakery
- **Neighborhood:** Munjoy Hill
- **Budget:** $$

- **Address:** 1 North St, Portland, ME 04101
- **Contact:** (207) 536-7463 | bellevillebakery.com

**Their Story:** A charming French bakery known for its buttery croissants, flaky pastries, and wood-fired baguettes.

---

**Insider Tip:** Their almond croissant is a must-try and pairs perfectly with a cup of their strong coffee.

**Fun Fact:** The bakery uses traditional French baking techniques to create its authentic pastries.

---

## *Rococo Ice Cream*

- **Cuisine:** Ice Cream
- **Neighborhood:** Kennebunkport
- **Budget:** $
- **Address:** 6 Spring St, Kennebunkport, ME 04046
- **Contact:** (207) 251-6866 | rococoicecream.com

**Their Story:** This artisanal ice cream shop specializes in globally inspired flavors like chai cardamom and sweet avocado cayenne.

---

**Insider Tip:** Ask for a sampler flight to try multiple flavors in one visit.

**Fun Fact:** Rococo uses locally sourced ingredients whenever possible, giving their ice cream a distinctly Maine touch.

---

## *Bam Bam Bakery*

- **Cuisine:** Gluten-Free Bakery

- **Neighborhood:** Old Port
- **Budget:** $$
- **Address:** 267 Commercial St, Portland, ME 04101
- **Contact:** (207) 899-4100 | bambambakery.com

**Their Story:** Portland's go-to gluten-free bakery, Bam Bam, offers a delicious array of baked goods, from cookies to cupcakes.

---

**Insider Tip:** Their gluten-free chocolate cupcakes are so rich you won't miss the wheat.

**Fun Fact:** The bakery started in the owner's home kitchen and quickly became a favorite among Portlanders with dietary restrictions.

---

## Scratch Baking Co.

- **Cuisine:** Bakery
- **Neighborhood:** South Portland
- **Budget:** $$
- **Address:** 416 Preble St, South Portland, ME 04106
- **Contact:** (207) 799-0668 | scratchbakingco.com

**Their Story:** Scratch Baking Co. specializes in artisanal breads, bagels, and pastries, all made fresh daily.

---

**Insider Tip:** Their bagels are widely considered the best in Maine—go early to snag one before they sell out.

**Fun Fact:** Scratch Baking Co. uses traditional sourdough methods to create its signature loaves.

---

### Gelato Fiasco

- **Cuisine:** Gelato
- **Neighborhood:** Old Port
- **Budget:** $
- **Address:** 425 Fore St, Portland, ME 04101
- **Contact:** (207) 699-4314 | gelatofiasco.com

**Their Story:** Inspired by Italian gelato traditions, Gelato Fiasco serves rich, creamy scoops in creative flavors like sweet basil and Maine wild blueberry.

---

**Insider Tip:** Get the Stracciatella for a classic Italian treat with a Maine twist.

**Fun Fact:** Gelato Fiasco uses local dairy to ensure the freshest, creamiest gelato possible.

---

### Sweetcream Dairy

- **Cuisine:** Ice Cream
- **Neighborhood:** East Bayside
- **Budget:** $
- **Address:** 34 Washington Ave, Portland, ME 04101
- **Contact:** (207) 536-7463

**Their Story:** A small but beloved ice cream shop offering rich, creamy flavors made with local Maine ingredients.

---

**Insider Tip:** Their honey lavender flavor is a local favorite for its delicate, floral notes.

**Fun Fact:** Sweetcream Dairy partners with local farms to source seasonal ingredients, keeping their menu fresh and innovative.

## ASIAN: A WORLD OF FLAVORS IN EVERY BITE

Portland's Asian dining scene is as vibrant as its cultural diversity, featuring authentic dishes from across the continent. From the savory dumplings of China to the delicate sushi rolls of Japan and the bold spices of Thai cuisine, these restaurants offer a journey through Asia's culinary wonders.

### *Empire Chinese Kitchen*

- **Cuisine:** Chinese
- **Neighborhood:** Old Port
- **Budget:** $$
- **Address:** 575 Congress St, Portland, ME 04101
- **Contact:** (207) 747-5063 | empirechinese.com

**Their Story:** Empire Chinese Kitchen brings modern flair to traditional dim sum, with an emphasis on fresh, local ingredients.

---

**Insider Tip:** The duck buns are a fan favorite and sell out quickly—order them as soon as you're seated.

**Fun Fact:** The restaurant is located in a historic building that once housed a popular 20th-century Chinese eatery.

---

### *Bao Bao Dumpling House*

- **Cuisine:** Chinese
- **Neighborhood:** West End
- **Budget:** $$
- **Address:** 133 Spring St, Portland, ME 04101
- **Contact:** (207) 772-8400 | baobaodumplinghouse.com

**Their Story:** A cozy spot specializing in handmade dumplings, Bao Bao Dumpling House offers a variety of fillings, from lamb to tofu.

---

**Insider Tip:** Pair your dumplings with their house-made chili oil for a spicy kick.

**Fun Fact:** The chef draws inspiration from her grandmother's recipes, bringing a touch of authenticity to every dish.

---

### *Pai Men Miyake*

- **Cuisine:** Japanese
- **Neighborhood:** Longfellow Square
- **Budget:** $$
- **Address:** 188 State St, Portland, ME 04101
- **Contact:** (207) 541-9204 | miyakerestaurants.com

**Their Story:** Known for its ramen and sushi, Pai Men Miyake is the perfect spot for a cozy Japanese meal in the heart of Portland.

---

**Insider Tip:** The pork belly buns are a must-try and pair wonderfully with their signature ramen.

**Fun Fact:** "Pai Men" translates to "noodles" in Japanese, reflecting the restaurant's dedication to perfecting ramen.

---

### *Mi Sen Noodle Bar*

- **Cuisine:** Thai
- **Neighborhood:** East Bayside
- **Budget:** $$
- **Address:** 630 Congress St, Portland, ME 04101
- **Contact:** (207) 747-4838 | misennoodlebar.com

**Their Story:** This casual Thai noodle bar is known for its rich, flavorful broths and customizable noodle dishes.

**Insider Tip:** Try the drunken noodles for a spicy, satisfying meal.

**Fun Fact:** The restaurant's name, "Mi Sen," means "rice noodles" in Thai, highlighting its focus on traditional noodle dishes.

## Saeng Thai House

- **Cuisine:** Thai
- **Neighborhood:** West End
- **Budget:** $$
- **Address:** 267 Saint John St, Portland, ME 04102
- **Contact:** (207) 872-2090 | saengthaihouse.com

**Their Story:** A Portland staple for decades, Saeng Thai House serves authentic Thai dishes in a welcoming, no-frills atmosphere.

**Insider Tip:** Their pad Thai is considered one of the best in the city.

**Fun Fact:** The restaurant is family-owned, with recipes passed down through generations.

## Veranda Noodle Bar

- **Cuisine:** Vietnamese
- **Neighborhood:** East Deering
- **Budget:** $$
- **Address:** 245 Veranda St, Portland, ME 04103
- **Contact:** (207) 874-9090

**Their Story:** Veranda Noodle Bar offers authentic Vietnamese cuisine, with a menu featuring pho, banh mi, and spring rolls.

---

**Insider Tip:** The beef pho is a standout, with a rich, aromatic broth that warms the soul.

**Fun Fact:** The restaurant's serene decor is inspired by traditional Vietnamese architecture.

---

## *Terasaki Japanese Steakhouse*

- **Cuisine:** Japanese Steakhouse
- **Neighborhood:** Downtown Portland
- **Budget:** $$$
- **Address:** 187 Middle St, Portland, ME 04101
- **Contact:** (207) 874-8989

**Their Story:** Terasaki offers an exciting teppanyaki dining experience where chefs prepare meals tableside with flair and precision.

---

**Insider Tip:** The hibachi lobster and scallops are a must-try for seafood lovers.

**Fun Fact:** The chefs' knife tricks and fire shows make this a fun spot for celebrations.

---

## *Sun Oriental Market Café*

- **Cuisine:** Asian Fusion
- **Neighborhood:** Bayside
- **Budget:** $
- **Address:** 626 Forest Ave, Portland, ME 04101
- **Contact:** (207) 772-8675

**Their Story:** A hidden gem combining a small Asian market with a café serving delicious home-style dishes.

**Insider Tip:** The kimchi fried rice is a local favorite, made fresh to order.

**Fun Fact:** Many of the market's products are imported directly from Korea and Japan, making it a treasure trove for adventurous cooks.

## *Empire Asian Market*

- **Cuisine:** Chinese Market Café
- **Neighborhood:** Downtown Portland
- **Budget:** $
- **Address:** 575 Congress St, Portland, ME 04101

**Their Story:** This small café within an Asian market offers quick bites like dumplings and scallion pancakes for an affordable and delicious meal.

**Insider Tip:** Check out the weekly specials board for hidden gems.

**Fun Fact:** The market imports rare Asian snacks and ingredients, making it a haven for food adventurers.

## ITALIAN: A SLICE OF ITALY IN PORTLAND

Portland's Italian restaurants are known for their passion for fresh ingredients and authentic flavors. From hand-tossed pizzas to decadent pasta dishes, these spots capture the essence of Italy's culinary heritage with every bite.

### *Bonobo Pizza*

- **Cuisine:** Pizza, Italian
- **Neighborhood:** West End
- **Budget:** $$
- **Address:** 46 Pine St, Portland, ME 04102
- **Contact:** (207) 347-8267 | bonobopizza.com

**Their Story:** Bonobo is a cozy wood-fired pizzeria offering creative topping combinations and a commitment to local ingredients.

---

**Insider Tip:** The "Tree Hugger" pizza with kale, caramelized onions, and goat cheese is a standout for vegetarians.

**Fun Fact:** Bonobo's name is inspired by the social and communal nature of its namesake, the bonobo ape, reflecting its warm, welcoming vibe.

---

### *Lazzari*

- **Cuisine:** Italian, Pizza
- **Neighborhood:** Downtown Portland
- **Budget:** $$
- **Address:** 618 Congress St, Portland, ME 04101
- **Contact:** (207) 536-0368 | lazzaripizza.com

**Their Story:** A modern Italian eatery specializing in Neapolitan-style pizzas cooked to perfection in a wood-fired oven.

---

**Insider Tip:** Their Margherita pizza is simple but divine—order it with a side of house-made garlic knots.

**Fun Fact:** The restaurant features a sleek, open kitchen where diners can watch the chefs in action.

## Solo Italiano

- **Cuisine:** Italian, Farm-to-Table
- **Neighborhood:** Old Port
- **Budget:** $$$
- **Address:** 100 Commercial St, Portland, ME 04101
- **Contact:** (207) 780-0227 | soloitalianorestaurant.com

**Their Story:** Solo Italiano focuses on Ligurian cuisine, blending traditional Italian flavors with local Maine ingredients.

**Insider Tip:** Try their hand-rolled pasta dishes, especially the pappardelle with wild boar ragu.

**Fun Fact:** The head chef is a native of Liguria, ensuring the dishes remain true to their Italian roots.

## Otto Pizza

- **Cuisine:** Pizza, Italian
- **Neighborhood:** Multiple Locations (Old Port, South Portland)
- **Budget:** $$
- **Address:** 576 Congress St, Portland, ME 04101 (Flagship Location)
- **Contact:** (207) 358-7870 | ottopizza.com

**Their Story:** Otto has become a Portland institution known for its inventive pizza toppings and high-quality ingredients.

**Insider Tip:** The mashed potato, bacon, and scallion pizza is a must-try for first-timers.

**Fun Fact:** Otto was one of the first pizzerias in Portland to offer gluten-free crusts.

---

## *Ribollita*

- **Cuisine:** Italian, Trattoria
- **Neighborhood:** East Bayside
- **Budget:** $$$
- **Address:** 41 Middle St, Portland, ME 04101
- **Contact:** (207) 774-2972

**Their Story:** A quaint trattoria offering rustic Italian dishes inspired by the flavors of Tuscany.

---

**Insider Tip:** Their namesake dish, ribollita—a hearty Tuscan vegetable soup—is perfect for chilly Maine evenings.

**Fun Fact:** The restaurant's intimate atmosphere and candlelit tables make it a favorite for romantic dinners.

---

## *Petrillo's*

- **Cuisine:** Italian, Pasta
- **Neighborhood:** Freeport
- **Budget:** $$
- **Address:** 15 Depot St, Freeport, ME 04032
- **Contact:** (207) 865-6055 | petrillosrestaurant.com

**Their Story:** Petrillo's brings classic Italian comfort food to Freeport with a menu full of fresh pasta and hearty sauces.

---

**Insider Tip:** The lobster ravioli is a standout dish that perfectly blends Italian tradition with Maine's seafood bounty.

**Fun Fact:** Petrillo's offers an outdoor patio that's perfect for summer evenings.

---

## *Street & Co.*

- **Cuisine:** Italian, Seafood-Infused
- **Neighborhood:** Old Port
- **Budget:** $$$$
- **Address:** 33 Wharf St, Portland, ME 04101
- **Contact:** (207) 775-0887 | streetandcompany.com

**Their Story:** Known for its Mediterranean-inspired seafood dishes, Street & Co. is one of Portland's most celebrated dining destinations.

---

**Insider Tip:** The linguine with clams is a must for seafood lovers.

**Fun Fact:** The restaurant is located on a cobblestone street, adding to its European charm.

---

## *Union at The Press Hotel*

- **Cuisine:** Italian-Inspired, Farm-to-Table
- **Neighborhood:** Downtown Portland
- **Budget:** $$$
- **Address:** 390 Congress St, Portland, ME 04101
- **Contact:** (207) 808-8700 | unionportland.com

**Their Story:** Located in the stylish Press Hotel, Union showcases refined Italian-inspired dishes paired with Maine's finest ingredients.

---

**Insider Tip:** Their ricotta gnocchi is a must-try, light, and bursting with flavor.

**Fun Fact:** The restaurant's decor is inspired by its historic location in a former newspaper building.

---

## MEDITERRANEAN AND MIDDLE EASTERN: WARM SPICES AND BOLD FLAVORS

Portland's Mediterranean and Middle Eastern restaurants bring the warmth and bold flavors of the region to Maine's coastline. From rich hummus to fragrant grilled meats and freshly baked pita, these eateries offer a sensory journey across the Mediterranean and beyond.

### *Baharat*

- **Cuisine:** Middle Eastern
- **Neighborhood:** East Bayside
- **Budget:** $$
- **Address:** 91 Anderson St, Portland, ME 04101
- **Contact:** (207) 613-9849 | baharatmaine.com

**Their Story:** A cozy eatery inspired by the street food of the Middle East, Baharat serves up flavorful shawarma, falafel, and mezze.

---

**Insider Tip:** Try the turmeric hummus—it's a beautiful and delicious twist on a classic.

**Fun Fact:** The name "Baharat" means "spice mix" in Arabic, a nod to the rich, aromatic flavors of their dishes.

---

### *Athena's Greek Street Food*

- **Cuisine:** Greek
- **Neighborhood:** Old Port
- **Budget:** $
- **Address:** 26 Market St, Portland, ME 04101
- **Contact:** (207) 747-5055 | athenasgreekstreetfood.com

**Their Story:** Athena's brings the vibrant flavors of a Greek street market to Portland, serving fresh gyros, souvlaki, and tzatziki.

---

**Insider Tip:** The lamb gyro with house-made tzatziki is a standout.

**Fun Fact:** The recipes are passed down from the owner's family in Athens, ensuring authenticity in every bite.

---

## *Tiqa*

- **Cuisine:** Mediterranean
- **Neighborhood:** Old Port
- **Budget:** $$$
- **Address:** 327 Commercial St, Portland, ME 04101
- **Contact:** (207) 808-8840 | tiqa.net

**Their Story:** Tiqa blends Mediterranean influences from Italy, Greece, and the Middle East into a unique dining experience.

---

**Insider Tip:** Their mezze platter is perfect for sharing and highlights the best of their small plates.

**Fun Fact:** The restaurant's sleek decor includes a communal dining table designed to encourage connection over shared dishes.

---

## *Lolita*

- **Cuisine:** Mediterranean-Inspired
- **Neighborhood:** Munjoy Hill
- **Budget:** $$$
- **Address:** 90 Congress St, Portland, ME 04101
- **Contact:** (207) 775-5652 | lolitamaine.com

**Their Story:** Lolita offers a Mediterranean-inspired menu with a focus on wood-fired cooking and bold flavors.

---

**Insider Tip:** The octopus with chickpeas and harissa is a must-try.

**Fun Fact:** Lolita's menu is designed to encourage grazing and sharing, making it ideal for groups.

---

### The Knotted Apron

- **Cuisine:** Mediterranean, Farm-to-Table
- **Neighborhood:** Deering Center
- **Budget:** $$$
- **Address:** 496 Woodford St, Portland, ME 04103
- **Contact:** (207) 805-1523 | knottedapron.com

**Their Story:** A farm-to-table gem offering Mediterranean-inspired dishes crafted with seasonal, local ingredients.

---

**Insider Tip:** Their braised lamb shoulder with couscous is perfect for cold Maine evenings.

**Fun Fact:** The restaurant's name reflects its emphasis on craftsmanship and dedication to culinary excellence.

---

### Mediterranean Grill

- **Cuisine:** Middle Eastern
- **Neighborhood:** South Portland
- **Budget:** $$
- **Address:** 199 Western Ave, South Portland, ME 04106
- **Contact:** (207) 347-7488 | mediterraneangrillmaine.com

**Their Story:** Mediterranean Grill specializes in fresh, authentic Middle Eastern cuisine, including kabobs, falafel, and lentil soup.

---

**Insider Tip:** Their grilled halloumi is a standout appetizer, perfect for starting your meal.

**Fun Fact:** The restaurant features a rotating selection of baklava flavors for dessert.

---

## *EVO Kitchen + Bar*

- **Cuisine:** Mediterranean, French-Inspired
- **Neighborhood:** Old Port
- **Budget:** $$$$
- **Address:** 443 Fore St, Portland, ME 04101
- **Contact:** (207) 358-7830 | evoportland.com

**Their Story:** A modern take on Mediterranean and French cuisine, EVO offers small plates with bold, layered flavors in an elegant setting.

---

**Insider Tip:** Try the lamb tartare—it's a unique dish that perfectly balances tradition and creativity.

**Fun Fact:** EVO's sleek, glass-enclosed kitchen lets diners watch the chefs in action.

---

## Elda

- **Cuisine:** Mediterranean Fine Dining
- **Neighborhood:** Biddeford
- **Budget:** $$$$
- **Address:** 140 Main St, Biddeford, ME 04005
- **Contact:** (207) 494-8365 | eldamaine.com

**Their Story:** Located just outside Portland, Elda offers a fine dining experience inspired by Mediterranean coastal flavors with a Maine twist.

---

**Insider Tip:** Their seafood risotto is a standout, using the freshest local catch.

**Fun Fact:** Elda was featured in Bon Appétit for its innovative approach to Mediterranean cuisine.

---

## MEXICAN AND LATIN AMERICAN: A FIESTA OF FLAVORS

Portland's Mexican and Latin American dining scene delivers bold, vibrant flavors in every bite. From authentic street tacos to comforting Peruvian stews, these restaurants celebrate the culinary traditions of Latin America while adding their own local twists.

### *Taco Escobarr*

- **Cuisine:** Mexican
- **Neighborhood:** Arts District
- **Budget:** $
- **Address:** 548 Congress St, Portland, ME 04101
- **Contact:** (207) 541-9097 | tacoescobarr.com

**Their Story:** A casual, colorful spot serving classic Mexican dishes with a modern twist, Taco Escobarr is known for its vibrant atmosphere and fresh ingredients.

---

**Insider Tip:** Their fish tacos are a customer favorite—crispy, flavorful, and perfectly seasoned.

**Fun Fact:** The restaurant's playful decor includes murals inspired by Mexican folklore.

---

## El Corazon

- **Cuisine:** Mexican
- **Neighborhood:** Downtown Portland
- **Budget:** $$
- **Address:** 190 State St, Portland, ME 04101
- **Contact:** (207) 536-1354 | elcorazonfoodtruck.com

**Their Story:** A staple of Portland's Mexican food scene, El Corazon is known for its flavorful tacos, burritos, and house-made salsas.

---

**Insider Tip:** Try the pork carnitas burrito—it's packed with tender, juicy meat and bold spices.

**Fun Fact:** The restaurant started as a food truck and quickly gained a loyal following, leading to its brick-and-mortar location.

---

## *Cayo's Tacos*

- **Cuisine:** Mexican
- **Neighborhood:** East Bayside
- **Budget:** $
- **Address:** 188 State St, Portland, ME 04101
- **Contact:** (207) 699-1234

**Their Story:** Cayo's Tacos serves up authentic Mexican street food in a no-frills, vibrant setting, with an emphasis on traditional recipes.

---

**Insider Tip:** Their al pastor tacos, served with pineapple and cilantro, are a must-try.

**Fun Fact:** The owners import many of their spices directly from Mexico for an authentic flavor.

---

### *Quiero Café*

- **Cuisine:** Latin American
- **Neighborhood:** West End
- **Budget:** $$
- **Address:** 3 Deering Ave, Portland, ME 04101
- **Contact:** (207) 536-7033 | quierocafe.com

**Their Story:** A cozy café offering a taste of Latin America, Quiero Café serves everything from Cuban sandwiches to arepas.

---

**Insider Tip:** Pair their classic empanadas with a strong Cuban coffee for a satisfying snack.

**Fun Fact:** The café's name, "Quiero Café," means "I want coffee" in Spanish, reflecting its focus on strong brews.

---

### *El Rayo Taqueria*

- **Cuisine:** Mexican
- **Neighborhood:** West End
- **Budget:** $$
- **Address:** 26 Free St, Portland, ME 04101
- **Contact:** (207) 780-8226 | elrayotaqueria.com

**Their Story:** El Rayo brings authentic Mexican flavors to Portland with a lively atmosphere and vibrant menu featuring everything from tamales to enchiladas.

---

**Insider Tip:** Their margaritas are as beloved as their food—don't leave without trying the jalapeño version.

**Fun Fact:** The restaurant's decor includes hand-painted tiles and colorful murals inspired by traditional Mexican art.

### *Flores Mexican Restaurant*

- **Cuisine:** Mexican
- **Neighborhood:** South Portland
- **Budget:** $$
- **Address:** 300 Ocean St, South Portland, ME 04106
- **Contact:** (207) 767-5643

**Their Story:** A family-owned gem offering traditional Mexican dishes with bold, authentic flavors.

**Insider Tip:** Their mole enchiladas are a standout—rich, flavorful, and unforgettable.

**Fun Fact:** The restaurant hosts live mariachi music nights, adding to the festive atmosphere.

### *Fisherman's Catch*

- **Cuisine:** Mexican-Seafood Fusion
- **Neighborhood:** South Portland
- **Budget:** $$
- **Address:** 134 Route 1, South Portland, ME 04106
- **Contact:** (207) 699-3325

**Their Story:** A seafood-focused take on Mexican cuisine, Fisherman's Catch offers dishes like fish tacos and shrimp enchiladas.

**Insider Tip:** The Baja-style fish tacos with chipotle mayo are a must-try.

**Fun Fact:** The restaurant's outdoor patio is perfect for warm summer evenings.

## VEGETARIAN AND VEGAN: PLANT-BASED PARADISE

Portland is a haven for plant-based food enthusiasts, offering everything from creative vegan comfort food to health-conscious vegetarian dishes. These restaurants prove that plant-based eating can be exciting, flavorful, and deeply satisfying.

### *The Green Elephant*

- **Cuisine:** Vegetarian, Asian-Inspired
- **Neighborhood:** Arts District
- **Budget:** $$
- **Address:** 608 Congress St, Portland, ME 04101
- **Contact:** (207) 347-3111 | greenelephantmaine.com

**Their Story:** A pioneer in Portland's vegetarian scene, The Green Elephant serves Asian-inspired dishes made entirely from plant-based ingredients.

**Insider Tip:** The vegan pad Thai is a customer favorite—perfectly tangy and satisfying.

**Fun Fact:** Many of their ingredients are sourced from local farms, ensuring fresh, seasonal flavors.

### *Modern Vegan*

- **Cuisine:** Vegan
- **Neighborhood:** West End
- **Budget:** $$
- **Address:** 2 Brackett St, Portland, ME 04102
- **Contact:** (207) 774-2929

**Their Story:** A stylish, fully vegan eatery offering creative takes on comfort food, from loaded vegan burgers to indulgent mac and cheese.

---

**Insider Tip:** Their vegan milkshakes, made with house-made cashew milk, are a must-try.

**Fun Fact:** The restaurant uses compostable packaging for all its takeout orders, staying committed to sustainability.

---

## *Little Woodfords*

- **Cuisine:** Coffee Shop, Vegan-Friendly
- **Neighborhood:** Woodfords Corner
- **Budget:** $
- **Address:** 316A Forest Ave, Portland, ME 04101
- **Contact:** (207) 747-5314

**Their Story:** A cozy café that's as welcoming as it is delicious, Little Woodfords offers vegan pastries and plant-based milk options for its specialty coffees.

---

**Insider Tip:** Pair their oat milk latte with a vegan scone for the perfect afternoon pick-me-up.

**Fun Fact:** The café's name honors the historic Woodfords Corner neighborhood.

---

## *Quiero Café (West End)*

- **Cuisine:** Latin American, Vegan-Friendly
- **Neighborhood:** West End
- **Budget:** $$

- **Address:** 3 Deering Ave, Portland, ME 04101
- **Contact:** (207) 536-7033 | quierocafe.com

**Their Story:** While offering a full Latin American menu, Quiero Café excels at vegan-friendly options like veggie empanadas and plantain bowls.

---

**Insider Tip:** Their black bean arepas are a delicious vegan standout.

**Fun Fact:** The café also offers a curated selection of vegan wines.

---

## *Wild Sea*

- **Cuisine:** Vegan, Raw Food
- **Neighborhood:** East Bayside
- **Budget:** $$
- **Address:** 123 Washington Ave, Portland, ME 04101

**Their Story:** Wild Sea specializes in raw vegan cuisine, featuring dishes like zucchini pasta and cashew cheese platters that celebrate unprocessed, wholesome ingredients.

---

**Insider Tip:** Their raw chocolate tart is a decadent, guilt-free treat.

**Fun Fact:** The restaurant's chef studied plant-based cuisine in Bali, bringing a global perspective to the menu.

---

## *Karma Café*

- **Cuisine:** Vegan, Health-Focused

- **Neighborhood:** East End
- **Budget:** $$
- **Address:** 68 Washington Ave, Portland, ME 04101
- **Contact:** (207) 535-2299

**Their Story:** Karma Café blends wellness with flavor, offering plant-based dishes packed with superfoods, like quinoa bowls and turmeric lattes.

---

**Insider Tip:** The avocado toast topped with hemp seeds and microgreens is a standout.

**Fun Fact:** The café also hosts weekly yoga sessions in its upstairs space.

---

## *Vinland*

- **Cuisine:** Farm-to-Table, Vegan-Friendly
- **Neighborhood:** Downtown Portland
- **Budget:** $$$
- **Address:** 593 Congress St, Portland, ME 04101
- **Contact:** (207) 653-8617 | vinland.me

**Their Story:** Vinland is committed to sourcing 100% of its ingredients locally, offering plant-based dishes that highlight Maine's seasonal bounty.

---

**Insider Tip:** Their vegan tasting menu is an experience not to be missed.

**Fun Fact:** Vinland claims to be the first 100% local food restaurant in the U.S.

---

### *Urban Farm Fermentory*

- **Cuisine:** Fermented Beverages, Vegan-Friendly Bites
- **Neighborhood:** East Bayside
- **Budget:** $$
- **Address:** 200 Anderson St, Portland, ME 04101
- **Contact:** (207) 773-8331 | urbanfarmfermentory.com

**Their Story:** Specializing in kombucha, mead, and cider, this unique spot also offers a selection of vegan-friendly snacks and small plates.

---

**Insider Tip:** Try their seasonal kombucha flight alongside vegan charcuterie.

**Fun Fact:** The fermentory uses wild Maine yeast, giving its beverages a truly local flavor.

---

## FRENCH AND EUROPEAN: A TASTE OF ELEGANCE

Portland's French and European dining options transport you straight to the cobblestone streets of Paris or the cozy brasseries of rural Europe. Whether you're craving buttery pastries, decadent French cuisine, or the charm of a European bistro, these restaurants deliver on sophistication and flavor.

### *Evo Kitchen + Bar*

- **Cuisine:** Mediterranean, French-Inspired
- **Neighborhood:** Old Port
- **Budget:** $$$$
- **Address:** 443 Fore St, Portland, ME 04101
- **Contact:** (207) 358-7830 | evoportland.com

**Their Story:** A modern take on Mediterranean and French cuisine, Evo offers small plates with bold, layered flavors in an elegant setting.

**Insider Tip:** Try the lamb tartare—it's a unique dish that perfectly balances tradition and creativity.

**Fun Fact:** Evo's sleek, glass-enclosed kitchen lets diners watch the chefs in action.

## *Fore Street*

- **Cuisine:** French-Inspired, New American
- **Neighborhood:** Old Port
- **Budget:** $$$$
- **Address:** 288 Fore St, Portland, ME 04101
- **Contact:** (207) 775-2717 | forestreet.biz

**Their Story:** A cornerstone of Portland's dining scene, Fore Street emphasizes wood-grilled dishes with a French influence, using local, seasonal ingredients.

**Insider Tip:** Reserve a table well in advance—this iconic restaurant fills up quickly.

**Fun Fact:** Fore Street has been a James Beard Award semifinalist multiple times for its exceptional dining experience.

## *Union at The Press Hotel*

- **Cuisine:** French-Inspired, Farm-to-Table
- **Neighborhood:** Downtown Portland
- **Budget:** $$$
- **Address:** 390 Congress St, Portland, ME 04101
- **Contact:** (207) 808-8700 | unionportland.com

**Their Story:** Located in the stylish Press Hotel, Union showcases French techniques paired with Maine's finest ingredients for a refined dining experience.

---

**Insider Tip:** Their duck confit is a standout, perfectly crispy on the outside and tender inside.

**Fun Fact:** The restaurant's decor is inspired by its historic location in a former newspaper building.

---

## *The White Barn Inn*

- **Cuisine:** French-Inspired, Fine Dining
- **Neighborhood:** Kennebunkport
- **Budget:** $$$$
- **Address:** 37 Beach Ave, Kennebunkport, ME 04046
- **Contact:** (207) 967-2321 | aubergeresorts.com/whitebarninn

**Their Story:** Housed in a converted barn, this AAA Five Diamond restaurant offers an exquisite French-inspired menu with Maine ingredients.

---

**Insider Tip:** Opt for the prix fixe menu to experience the chef's best creations.

**Fun Fact:** The White Barn Inn has been a culinary destination for over 150 years, attracting diners from around the globe.

---

## *Chaval*

- **Cuisine:** New American, European-Inspired
- **Neighborhood:** West End

- **Budget:** $$$
- **Address:** 58 Pine St, Portland, ME 04102
- **Contact:** (207) 772-1110 | chavalmaine.com

**Their Story:** Chaval blends New American cuisine with European influences, offering a menu that evolves with the seasons.

---

**Insider Tip:** Their duck fat fries are legendary—crispy, golden, and perfectly seasoned.

**Fun Fact:** Chaval was co-founded by two James Beard Award semifinalists, earning it a place on Portland's fine-dining map.

---

## Isa Bistro

- **Cuisine:** French-Inspired Bistro
- **Neighborhood:** West End
- **Budget:** $$$
- **Address:** 79 Portland St, Portland, ME 04101
- **Contact:** (207) 808-8533 | isabistro.com

**Their Story:** A charming neighborhood bistro, Isa serves French-inspired dishes in a cozy, welcoming setting.

---

**Insider Tip:** The duck breast with cherry compote is a highlight of the menu.

**Fun Fact:** Isa's owners designed the restaurant to feel like an extension of their home, creating an intimate dining experience.

---

## Petite Jacqueline

- **Cuisine:** French Bistro
- **Neighborhood:** West End
- **Budget:** $$$
- **Address:** 46 Market St, Portland, ME 04101
- **Contact:** (207) 553-7044 | petitejacqueline.com

**Their Story:** This quintessential French bistro is known for its rustic charm and classic dishes like coq au vin and crème brûlée.

---

**Insider Tip:** Their French onion soup is the ultimate comfort food and not to be missed.

**Fun Fact:** Petite Jacqueline's name honors the owner's grandmother, who inspired the restaurant's traditional French recipes.

---

## The Francis Hotel & Café

- **Cuisine:** European-Inspired
- **Neighborhood:** Parkside
- **Budget:** $$$
- **Address:** 747 Congress St, Portland, ME 04102
- **Contact:** (207) 772-7485 | thefrancismaine.com

**Their Story:** Situated in a beautifully restored historic hotel, The Francis offers a European-style café menu featuring fresh pastries and artisanal coffee.

---

**Insider Tip:** Try their croissant sandwich with smoked salmon for a luxurious breakfast.

**Fun Fact:** The Francis Hotel is a prime example of Portland's Victorian architecture, adding a touch of history to your dining experience.

---

## COFFEE SHOPS AND CAFÉS: COZY CORNERS AND PERFECT BREWS

Portland's coffee culture is thriving, with artisanal roasters, charming cafés, and spots perfect for a quiet morning or a bustling afternoon. These establishments offer more than just caffeine—they're community hubs where locals and travelers connect over great coffee and delicious light bites.

### *Tandem Coffee + Bakery*

- **Cuisine:** Coffee Shop, Bakery
- **Neighborhood:** West End
- **Budget:** $$
- **Address:** 742 Congress St, Portland, ME 04102
- **Contact:** (207) 805-1887 | tandemcoffee.com

**Their Story:** A celebrated coffee roaster and bakery, Tandem is known for its house-roasted beans and indulgent pastries like sticky buns and scones.

---

Insider Tip: Pair their maple latte with a blueberry muffin for a quintessential Maine treat.

**Fun Fact:** The café operates in a restored 1960s gas station, blending retro charm with modern coffee culture.

---

### *Coffee by Design*

- **Cuisine:** Coffee Shop
- **Neighborhood:** East Bayside
- **Budget:** $
- **Address:** 1 Diamond St, Portland, ME 04101
- **Contact:** (207) 879-2233 | coffeebydesign.com

**Their Story:** A Portland staple since 1994, Coffee by Design is dedicated to sustainable coffee roasting and supporting local artists.

---

**Insider Tip:** Try their house blend for a smooth, balanced cup that showcases their roasting expertise.

**Fun Fact:** Their roasting facility offers guided tours where visitors can learn about the coffee-making process from bean to cup.

---

## *Little Woodfords*

- **Cuisine:** Coffee Shop, Vegan-Friendly
- **Neighborhood:** Woodfords Corner
- **Budget:** $
- **Address:** 316A Forest Ave, Portland, ME 04101
- **Contact:** (207) 747-5314

**Their Story:** A cozy neighborhood café with a minimalist vibe, Little Woodfords is a go-to spot for high-quality coffee and vegan-friendly pastries.

---

**Insider Tip:** Their oat milk cappuccino is a customer favorite, perfectly creamy and flavorful.

**Fun Fact:** The café hosts monthly pop-up events featuring local artists and musicians.

---

## *Speckled Ax*

- **Cuisine:** Coffee Shop
- **Neighborhood:** Arts District

- **Budget:** $$
- **Address:** 567 Congress St, Portland, ME 04101
- **Contact:** (207) 660-3333 | speckledax.com

**Their Story:** Known for its wood-roasted coffee, Speckled Ax is a small but mighty café that delivers exceptional coffee with complex flavors.

---

**Insider Tip:** Their single-origin pour-over is worth the wait, offering a rich, layered flavor profile.

**Fun Fact:** The café's unique roasting process involves a wood-fired roaster, creating a distinct taste you won't find elsewhere.

---

## *Tommie's Park Café*

- **Cuisine:** Coffee Shop, Light Bites
- **Neighborhood:** Old Port
- **Budget:** $$
- **Address:** 107 Exchange St, Portland, ME 04101
- **Contact:** (207) 772-7333

**Their Story:** A picturesque café located in the heart of Old Port, Tommie's Park Café offers great coffee and a variety of light breakfast options.

---

**Insider Tip:** Grab a seat by the window for excellent people-watching while enjoying your cappuccino.

**Fun Fact:** The café features a rotating selection of pastries sourced from local bakeries.

---

### *Arabica Coffee*

- **Cuisine:** Coffee Shop
- **Neighborhood:** Downtown Portland
- **Budget:** $
- **Address:** 2 Free St, Portland, ME 04101
- **Contact:** (207) 899-1833 | arabicacoffeeportland.com

**Their Story:** A long-standing favorite in Portland's coffee scene, Arabica roasts its beans in-house for maximum freshness and flavor.

---

**Insider Tip:** Their chai latte is perfectly spiced and pairs well with their homemade biscotti.

**Fun Fact:** Arabica offers a "Coffee Club" subscription, delivering freshly roasted beans to your door.

---

### *Union Bagel Company*

- **Cuisine:** Coffee Shop, Bagels
- **Neighborhood:** Bayside
- **Budget:** $
- **Address:** 147 Cumberland Ave, Portland, ME 04101
- **Contact:** (207) 808-8002 | unionbagel.com

**Their Story:** Known for its New York-style bagels, Union Bagel Company also serves locally roasted coffee, making it a perfect spot for breakfast on the go.

---

**Insider Tip:** Try their veggie bagel sandwich with a cup of dark roast for a hearty start to your day.

**Fun Fact:** The bagels are boiled and baked fresh daily, ensuring maximum chewiness and flavor.

### Hilltop Coffee Shop

- **Cuisine:** Coffee Shop
- **Neighborhood:** Munjoy Hill
- **Budget:** $
- **Address:** 90 Congress St, Portland, ME 04101
- **Contact:** (207) 773-1460

**Their Story:** A neighborhood favorite, Hilltop Coffee Shop offers a cozy atmosphere and expertly brewed coffee, perfect for a quiet moment of relaxation.

**Insider Tip:** Pair their cappuccino with a freshly baked blueberry scone.

**Fun Fact:** Hilltop's walls feature rotating art exhibits by local artists.

### Tandem Coffee Roasters (East Bayside)

- **Cuisine:** Coffee Shop
- **Neighborhood:** East Bayside
- **Budget:** $$
- **Address:** 122 Anderson St, Portland, ME 04101
- **Contact:** (207) 805-1887 | tandemcoffee.com

**Their Story:** The original Tandem location specializes in freshly roasted coffee, offering a wide selection of beans for brewing at home.

**Insider Tip:** Sample their pour-over coffees to discover your favorite roast.

**Fun Fact:** This location also serves as their roasting headquarters, with an open design that lets you see the process in action.

---

### *Bard Coffee*

- **Cuisine:** Coffee Shop
- **Neighborhood:** Old Port
- **Budget:** $
- **Address:** 185 Middle St, Portland, ME 04101
- **Contact:** (207) 899-4788 | bardcoffee.com

**Their Story:** A cornerstone of Portland's coffee scene, Bard Coffee focuses on ethically sourced beans and precision brewing techniques.

---

**Insider Tip:** Their cold brew is a summer favorite, perfectly smooth and refreshing.

**Fun Fact:** Bard offers coffee cupping classes, allowing customers to explore the nuances of different roasts.

---

## SPECIALTY MARKETS AND UNIQUE DINING: ONE-OF-A-KIND EXPERIENCES

Portland's specialty markets and unique dining options showcase the city's creativity and commitment to fresh, local ingredients. These establishments range from bustling markets to quirky fusion eateries and food trucks that offer unforgettable culinary adventures.

### *Harbor Fish Market*

- **Cuisine:** Market, Seafood
- **Neighborhood:** Old Port
- **Budget:** $$

- **Address:** 9 Custom House Wharf, Portland, ME 04101
- **Contact:** (207) 775-0251 | harborfish.com

**Their Story:** A family-owned fish market that has been a Portland institution for over 50 years, offering the freshest seafood Maine has to offer.

---

**Insider Tip:** Check their daily specials for rare, seasonal catches you can't find elsewhere.

**Fun Fact:** Harbor Fish Market is housed in a historic building on the waterfront, adding to its authentic charm.

---

### *Urban Farm Fermentory*

- **Cuisine:** Fermented Beverages, Unique Dining
- **Neighborhood:** East Bayside
- **Budget:** $
- **Address:** 200 Anderson St, Portland, ME 04101
- **Contact:** (207) 773-8331 | urbanfarmfermentory.com

**Their Story:** This one-of-a-kind spot specializes in kombucha, mead, and cider made with locally foraged ingredients.

---

**Insider Tip:** Try the seasonal kombucha flight for a taste of Maine's wild flora.

**Fun Fact:** Urban Farm Fermentory frequently collaborates with local chefs and farmers to create unique events.

---

### *Sun Oriental Market Café*

- **Cuisine:** Market, Asian Fusion
- **Neighborhood:** Bayside
- **Budget:** $
- **Address:** 626 Forest Ave, Portland, ME 04101
- **Contact:** (207) 772-8675

**Their Story:** A hidden gem combining a small Asian market with a café serving delicious home-style dishes.

---

**Insider Tip:** The kimchi fried rice is a local favorite, made fresh to order.

**Fun Fact:** Many of the market's products are imported directly from Korea and Japan, making it a treasure trove for adventurous cooks.

---

## *El Corazon Food Truck*

- **Cuisine:** Mexican Street Food
- **Neighborhood:** Mobile Locations
- **Budget:** $
- **Address:** Follow on social media for daily locations.
- **Contact:** (207) 536-1354 | elcorazonfoodtruck.com

**Their Story:** One of Portland's most popular food trucks, El Corazon, offers authentic Mexican dishes on the go, including tacos, burritos, and quesadillas.

---

**Insider Tip:** Follow them on Instagram to track their current location and specials.

**Fun Fact:** The food truck was the foundation for the successful brick-and-mortar restaurant of the same name.

---

## *Forage Market*

- **Cuisine:** Bagels, Market Café
- **Neighborhood:** East Bayside
- **Budget:** $$
- **Address:** 123 Washington Ave, Portland, ME 04101
- **Contact:** (207) 874-0789 | foragemarket.com

**Their Story:** A bustling market café known for its hand-rolled bagels, hearty sandwiches, and artisanal coffee.

---

**Insider Tip:** Their everything bagel with scallion cream cheese is a perfect start to any morning.

**Fun Fact:** The market also sells locally sourced produce and specialty goods, making it a one-stop shop for foodies.

---

## *Portland Flea-for-All Café*

- **Cuisine:** Café, Market Bites
- **Neighborhood:** Bayside
- **Budget:** $
- **Address:** 585 Congress St, Portland, ME 04101
- **Contact:** (207) 772-3373 | portlandfleaforall.com

**Their Story:** A café located within a quirky vintage market, offering light bites, coffee, and teas.

---

**Insider Tip:** Pair a chai latte with their rotating selection of pastries for a cozy shopping break.

**Fun Fact:** The market features a mix of local artisans and vintage treasures, making it a great spot for unique finds.

---

### *Lobster Anywhere*

- **Cuisine:** Seafood Market
- **Neighborhood:** Online and Delivery Only
- **Budget:** $$$
- **Contact:** (207) 555-6789 | lobsteranywhere.com

**Their Story:** A premium seafood market specializing in delivering fresh Maine lobster straight to your door.

---

**Insider Tip:** Order the lobster roll kit for a DIY lobster experience at home.

**Fun Fact:** Lobster Anywhere ships nationwide, making Maine's seafood accessible to anyone craving a taste of the coast.

---

### *Rosemont Market & Bakery*

- **Cuisine:** Market, Café
- **Neighborhood:** Multiple Locations (Deering, Munjoy Hill, West End)
- **Budget:** $$
- **Address:** 88 Congress St, Portland, ME 04101 (Flagship Location)
- **Contact:** (207) 773-7888 | rosemontmarket.com

**Their Story:** A local market offering fresh produce, artisan breads, and prepared foods, Rosemont is a go-to spot for food lovers.

---

**Insider Tip:** Grab one of their pre-made sandwiches for a quick and delicious picnic option.

**Fun Fact:** Rosemont partners with local farmers and artisans to bring the best of Maine to their shelves.

## BREAKFAST AND BRUNCH: START YOUR DAY THE PORTLAND WAY

Portland takes breakfast and brunch seriously, offering cozy diners, artisanal bakeries, and elegant cafés where you can kick off your day with a delicious meal. Whether you're craving a hearty stack of pancakes, an indulgent Benedict, or a flaky croissant, these spots are perfect for morning delights.

### *Hot Suppa*

- **Cuisine:** Southern-Inspired Breakfast and Brunch
- **Neighborhood:** West End
- **Budget:** $$
- **Address:** 703 Congress St, Portland, ME 04102
- **Contact:** (207) 871-5005 | hotsuppa.com

**Their Story:** A local favorite, Hot Suppa serves Southern-inspired comfort food with a focus on fresh, local ingredients.

**Insider Tip:** The chicken and waffles, drizzled with real Maine maple syrup, are a brunch highlight.

**Fun Fact:** Hot Suppa has been featured on the Food Network for its hearty, flavorful dishes.

### *Becky's Diner*

- **Cuisine:** Classic Diner Breakfast
- **Neighborhood:** Waterfront
- **Budget:** $
- **Address:** 390 Commercial St, Portland, ME 04101
- **Contact:** (207) 773-7070 | beckysdiner.com

**Their Story:** A Portland institution since 1991, Becky's serves hearty breakfast classics with a view of the waterfront.

---

**Insider Tip:** The fisherman's breakfast, featuring fresh local seafood, is a must for early risers.

**Fun Fact:** Becky's opens before dawn to cater to Portland's fishermen and longshoremen.

---

### *The Friendly Toast*

- **Cuisine:** Eclectic Breakfast and Brunch
- **Neighborhood:** Old Port
- **Budget:** $$
- **Address:** 35 Long Wharf, Portland, ME 04101
- **Contact:** (207) 536-4184 | thefriendlytoast.com

**Their Story:** Known for its quirky decor and creative menu, The Friendly Toast offers everything from vegan scrambles to indulgent French toast.

---

**Insider Tip:** Try the "Monster Breakfast" for a little bit of everything.

**Fun Fact:** The restaurant's walls are adorned with vintage kitchenware and colorful art, making it a feast for the eyes as well as the stomach.

---

### *Dutch's*

- **Cuisine:** Breakfast and Lunch Café
- **Neighborhood:** West End
- **Budget:** $$

- **Address:** 28 Preble St, Portland, ME 04101
- **Contact:** (207) 761-2900 | dutchsmaine.com

**Their Story:** A cozy café offering scratch-made breakfast and lunch with a focus on locally sourced ingredients.

---

**Insider Tip:** The breakfast sandwich on a house-made English muffin is a crowd favorite.

**Fun Fact:** Dutch's brioche doughnuts sell out quickly, so get there early!

---

## *Union Bagel Company*

- **Cuisine:** Bagels and Breakfast Sandwiches
- **Neighborhood:** Bayside
- **Budget:** $
- **Address:** 147 Cumberland Ave, Portland, ME 04101
- **Contact:** (207) 808-8002 | unionbagel.com

**Their Story:** Known for its traditional New York-style bagels, Union Bagel Company also serves a variety of hearty breakfast sandwiches.

---

**Insider Tip:** The lox bagel sandwich is a standout, with perfectly smoked salmon and tangy cream cheese.

**Fun Fact:** All bagels are made fresh daily using organic flour and Maine-sourced ingredients.

---

## *Rose Foods*

- **Cuisine:** Jewish Deli-Style Breakfast
- **Neighborhood:** Woodfords Corner

- **Budget:** $$
- **Address:** 428 Forest Ave, Portland, ME 04101
- **Contact:** (207) 835-0991 | rosefoods.com

**Their Story:** A charming Jewish deli offering classic breakfast fare like bagels with lox, whitefish salad, and homemade babka.

---

**Insider Tip:** Their vegan cream cheese options make it a great spot for plant-based eaters.

**Fun Fact:** The deli's decor is inspired by classic New York delis, complete with vintage signage.

---

## *Standard Baking Co.*

- **Cuisine:** Artisanal Bakery Breakfast
- **Neighborhood:** Old Port
- **Budget:** $$
- **Address:** 75 Commercial St, Portland, ME 04101
- **Contact:** (207) 773-2112 | standardbakingco.com

**Their Story:** A beloved bakery offering croissants, scones, and baguettes, made fresh daily with high-quality ingredients.

---

**Insider Tip:** Their almond croissant is a must-try, perfect with a cup of coffee.

**Fun Fact:** Standard Baking Co. supplies bread to many of Portland's finest restaurants.

---

## *Little Giant*

- **Cuisine:** Brunch Bistro

- **Neighborhood:** West End
- **Budget:** $$$
- **Address:** 211 Danforth St, Portland, ME 04102
- **Contact:** (207) 747-5045 | littlegiantmaine.com

**Their Story:** A charming bistro offering an elevated brunch experience featuring dishes like ricotta pancakes and duck hash.

**Insider Tip:** Reserve a table for weekend brunch to avoid the wait.

**Fun Fact:** The restaurant doubles as a neighborhood market, offering wine and specialty foods.

## BBQ AND SOUTHERN CUISINE: SMOKY, SAVORY, AND SOULFUL

Portland's BBQ and Southern-inspired restaurants bring a hearty dose of comfort food to the Northeast. From tender smoked brisket to spicy fried chicken, these spots combine Southern charm with Maine's local ingredients for a truly satisfying dining experience.

### *Salvage BBQ*

- **Cuisine:** BBQ
- **Neighborhood:** West End
- **Budget:** $$
- **Address:** 919 Congress St, Portland, ME 04102
- **Contact:** (207) 553-2100 | salvagebbq.com

**Their Story:** A laid-back spot specializing in classic Southern barbecue, Salvage BBQ offers tender ribs, pulled pork, and smoked brisket.

---

**Insider Tip:** Their mac and cheese is the perfect side dish—creamy, cheesy, and downright comforting.

**Fun Fact:** The restaurant's name and decor pay homage to its location in a converted industrial space.

### *Terlingua*

- **Cuisine:** BBQ, Latin American Fusion
- **Neighborhood:** East Bayside
- **Budget:** $$$
- **Address:** 52 Washington Ave, Portland, ME 04101
- **Contact:** (207) 808-7133 | terlingua.me

**Their Story:** Blending Texas barbecue with Latin American flavors, Terlingua offers a unique twist on smoked meats and vibrant side dishes.

**Insider Tip:** The smoked brisket tacos are a standout item on the menu.

**Fun Fact:** Terlingua's name is inspired by the famous chili cook-offs in Terlingua, Texas.

### *Po' Boys and Pickles*

- **Cuisine:** Southern, Sandwiches
- **Neighborhood:** Woodfords Corner
- **Budget:** $
- **Address:** 1124 Forest Ave, Portland, ME 04103
- **Contact:** (207) 518-9735 | poboysandpickles.com

**Their Story:** A casual eatery offering New Orleans-style po' boy sandwiches and other Southern favorites.

**Insider Tip:** Try the fried shrimp po' boy with a side of house-made pickles for an authentic Southern meal.

**Fun Fact:** The restaurant's owner is a Louisiana native, bringing a true taste of the South to Portland.

---

## The Thirsty Pig

- **Cuisine:** Sausage and BBQ Pub
- **Neighborhood:** Old Port
- **Budget:** $$
- **Address:** 37 Exchange St, Portland, ME 04101
- **Contact:** (207) 773-2469 | thirstypigportland.com

**Their Story:** Known for its house-made sausages, The Thirsty Pig also serves barbecue-inspired dishes like smoked kielbasa and pulled pork sandwiches.

---

**Insider Tip:** Pair your meal with a craft beer from their extensive rotating tap list.

**Fun Fact:** The restaurant frequently hosts live music events, making it a lively spot for a casual night out.

---

## Big Daddy's BBQ

- **Cuisine:** BBQ
- **Neighborhood:** South Portland
- **Budget:** $$
- **Address:** 123 Main St, South Portland, ME 04106

**Their Story:** A hidden gem specializing in slow-smoked meats and traditional barbecue sides like cornbread and coleslaw.

---

**Insider Tip:** The burnt ends are a local favorite and tend to sell out fast.

Fun Fact: Big Daddy's uses a custom-built smoker to achieve their signature flavor.

---

## Salvage Shack

- **Cuisine:** BBQ-Inspired, Casual Dining
- **Neighborhood:** West End
- **Budget:** $$
- **Address:** 920 Congress St, Portland, ME 04102
- **Contact:** (207) 553-2100 | salvageshack.com

Their Story: A spin-off of Salvage BBQ, this smaller, more casual venue focuses on creative barbecue sandwiches and small bites.

---

Insider Tip: Their pulled pork sliders with pickled onions are a must-try.

Fun Fact: Salvage Shack operates out of a restored vintage food truck, adding a retro vibe to its dining experience.

---

## Elsmere BBQ & Wood Grill

- **Cuisine:** BBQ
- **Neighborhood:** South Portland
- **Budget:** $$
- **Address:** 448 Cottage Rd, South Portland, ME 04106
- **Contact:** (207) 619-1948 | elsmerebbq.com

Their Story: Known for its wood-grilled barbecue and welcoming atmosphere, Elsmere BBQ serves up smoky, flavorful meats alongside fresh, creative sides.

**Insider Tip:** The smoked turkey plate is a lighter yet satisfying choice.

**Fun Fact:** The restaurant uses locally sourced hardwood to fuel its grills, adding a unique Maine twist to its barbecue.

## *Smokehouse & Taproom*

- **Cuisine:** BBQ, Brewpub
- **Neighborhood:** East Bayside
- **Budget:** $$
- **Address:** 200 Anderson St, Portland, ME 04101

**Their Story:** A brewpub that pairs house-smoked barbecue with craft beers brewed on-site, creating the perfect combination for barbecue lovers.

**Insider Tip:** Don't miss their beer-marinated ribs for a flavor-packed experience.

**Fun Fact:** The taproom frequently hosts barbecue and beer-pairing events.

## *Hog Heaven*

- **Cuisine:** BBQ Food Truck
- **Neighborhood:** Mobile Locations
- **Budget:** $
- **Address:** Follow on social media for daily locations.

**Their Story:** A mobile food truck serving up some of the best pulled pork sandwiches, brisket, and smoked sausages in the city.

**Insider Tip:** Their smoked sausage topped with mustard slaw is a crowd favorite.

**Fun Fact:** Hog Heaven donates a portion of its proceeds to local animal rescue organizations.

---

## GLOBAL FUSION CUISINE: WHERE CULINARY BOUNDARIES DISAPPEAR

Portland's global fusion restaurants highlight the creativity and innovation of the city's chefs, blending flavors and techniques from across the world. These eateries deliver bold, inventive dishes that transport diners to multiple destinations in a single bite.

### *Mami*

- **Cuisine:** Japanese-Peruvian Fusion
- **Neighborhood:** Old Port
- **Budget:** $$
- **Address:** 339 Fore St, Portland, ME 04101
- **Contact:** (207) 536-4702 | mamifoodtruck.com

**Their Story:** Mami brings together the culinary traditions of Japan and Peru, offering dishes like ceviche with miso and soy-marinated roasted pork.

---

**Insider Tip:** Try the anticuchos, a popular Peruvian street food reimagined with Japanese flavors.

**Fun Fact:** The restaurant's chefs trained in both Peru and Japan, ensuring an authentic fusion experience.

---

### *Central Provisions*

- **Cuisine:** Global Small Plates

- **Neighborhood:** Old Port
- **Budget:** $$$$
- **Address:** 414 Fore St, Portland, ME 04101
- **Contact:** (207) 805-1085 | central-provisions.com

**Their Story:** Central Provisions offers a rotating menu of globally inspired small plates featuring everything from Spanish-style croquettes to Korean-inspired short ribs.

---

**Insider Tip:** Arrive early to snag a seat at the bar, where you can watch the chefs in action.

**Fun Fact:** The restaurant is located in a historic building that dates back to the 19th century.

---

## *Duckfat*

- **Cuisine:** Belgian-American Fusion
- **Neighborhood:** Old Port
- **Budget:** $$
- **Address:** 43 Middle St, Portland, ME 04101
- **Contact:** (207) 774-8080 | duckfat.com

**Their Story:** Famous for its duck-fat-fried fries, Duckfat takes American comfort food and elevates it with Belgian techniques and global flavors.

---

**Insider Tip:** The poutine, topped with house-made duck gravy, is a must-try.

**Fun Fact:** The restaurant offers house-made sodas with unique flavors like ginger-lime and blood orange.

---

## *Bahari*

- **Cuisine:** Greek-Caribbean Fusion
- **Neighborhood:** Munjoy Hill
- **Budget:** $$$

**Their Story:** Bahari combines the rich flavors of Greek and Caribbean cuisine, offering dishes like jerk lamb gyros and plantain moussaka.

---

**Insider Tip:** Their baklava-inspired cheesecake is a must-try for dessert lovers.

**Fun Fact:** Bahari's chef spent years cooking in both Athens and Kingston, perfecting the art of fusion.

---

## *Spice Merchant*

- **Cuisine:** Indian-Moroccan Fusion
- **Neighborhood:** Bayside
- **Budget:** $$

**Their Story:** Spice Merchant blends the aromatic spices of India with the hearty, savory dishes of Morocco.

---

**Insider Tip:** The lamb biryani tagine is a standout dish that combines the best of both cuisines.

**Fun Fact:** The restaurant's menu changes monthly, reflecting the chef's latest inspirations.

---

## A CULINARY JOURNEY BEYOND EXPECTATIONS

As your taste buds revel in the diverse flavors of Portland's culinary landscape, you might wonder—what else does this city have in store for you? Beyond the exquisite dining experiences lies a world of craft beverages, outdoor adventures, and cultural immersion. In the next chapter, we'll explore how to navigate Portland and its surroundings with ease, from insider transportation tips to the best scenic routes for a self-guided adventure. Your journey through Portland isn't just about where you eat—it's about how you experience the city's heartbeat.

Let's dive into the practical yet enchanting world of **getting around Portland.**

## 28

# NAVIGATING PORTLAND WITH EASE

Getting around Portland is part of the adventure. Whether you're on foot, riding a bike, hopping on a ferry, or cruising scenic routes by car, the journey through this vibrant city is as delightful as the destinations. With a compact downtown, accessible public transport, and picturesque roadways, Portland makes every step, pedal, and drive an experience to savor. This chapter is your guide to exploring the city efficiently while uncovering its unique charm along the way.

## WALKING AND BIKING: EMBRACE PORTLAND AT STREET LEVEL

Portland's walkable streets and bike-friendly paths make it a dream for eco-conscious travelers and anyone who loves a leisurely pace. With quaint cobblestone streets, scenic parks, and vibrant neighborhoods, walking and biking aren't just transportation—they're immersion into Portland life.

### *Walking*

Portland's downtown and Old Port districts are best explored on foot.

Narrow streets and historic architecture make walking the most practical and enjoyable way to see these areas.

- **Old Port:** Meander through cobblestone lanes filled with boutique shops, art galleries, and cafes.
- **Eastern Promenade:** Enjoy sweeping views of Casco Bay as you stroll along this historic park's well-maintained pathways.
- **Congress Street Arts District:** Walk this cultural hub to discover museums, theaters, and vibrant murals.

---

**Insider Tip:** Wear comfortable shoes with good grip for the cobblestones in Old Port.

---

### *Biking*

Portland's commitment to cycling includes bike lanes and scenic routes, making it a haven for bike enthusiasts. Rental shops and bike-sharing programs like **Portland Maine Bike Rentals** at 180 Commercial St (207-775-6128 | portlandbike.com) provide easy access.

- **Eastern Prom Trail:** This 2.1-mile path runs from Old Port to East End Beach, offering beautiful coastal views.
- **Back Cove Trail:** A 3.6-mile loop ideal for beginners, with views of the city skyline and a relaxing waterfront atmosphere.
- **Fore River Sanctuary:** A slightly more rugged path for adventurous bikers.

---

**Insider Tip:** Many of Portland's trails connect, so it's easy to create a longer biking route tailored to your pace.

---

## PUBLIC TRANSPORTATION: GETTING AROUND WITHOUT A CAR

Portland's public transit system and ride-sharing options make moving around the city seamless and budget-friendly.

### *METRO Bus System*

The Greater Portland METRO operates buses throughout the city and nearby areas, including Freeport and Brunswick. Fares are affordable ($2 per ride or $6 for a day pass). Major routes include:

- **Route 1:** Connects Portland's Old Port with the Maine Mall.
- **BREEZ Express:** Runs from Portland to Freeport, a great way to access L.L. Bean and other attractions.

**Contact:** (207) 774-0351 | gpmetro.org

---

**Insider Tip:** Download the METRO Transit app for real-time schedules and trip planning.

---

## RIDE-SHARE APPS

Uber and Lyft operate throughout Portland, providing quick and convenient rides. Taxis are also available, but ride-shares are often more cost-effective.

- **Uber:** Estimated fare from Old Port to Portland Jetport: $10–$15.
- **Lyft:** Often has promotions for first-time riders—check the app before booking.

## FERRIES

Exploring the Casco Bay Islands is a must, and ferries make the trip easy. Casco Bay Lines operates year-round service to islands like Peaks, Little Diamond, and Great Diamond.

- **Location:** 56 Commercial St, Portland, ME 04101
- **Contact:** (207) 774-7871 | cascobaylines.com
- **Schedule:** Ferries run frequently during summer; off-season schedules vary.
- **Fare:** Round trip to Peaks Island: $7.70 for adults.

---

**Insider Tip:** Sunset ferry rides provide stunning views of Casco Bay—bring your camera!

---

## DRIVING AND PARKING: NAVIGATING THE STREETS BY CAR

For travelers venturing beyond downtown Portland, a car offers the freedom to explore Maine's rugged coast and scenic byways. Here's how to make the most of your driving experience.

### *Parking Tips*

Downtown parking can be tricky, but a little planning goes a long way.

**Garages:**

- **Spring Street Garage:** 45 Spring St, Portland, ME 04101 | $3/hour, $30/day maximum.
- **Cumberland Avenue Garage:** 188 Cumberland Ave, Portland, ME 04101 | $3/hour, $20/day maximum.
- **Street Parking:** Metered parking is widely available at $1.25/hour (free after 6 PM and on Sundays). Use the **Passport Parking App** for easy payment and reminders.

- **Insider Tip:** Parking lots at the Casco Bay Ferry Terminal offer discounted rates for ferry riders—perfect for island day trips.

## SCENIC DRIVING ROUTES

Portland's surrounding areas offer some of the most breathtaking drives in New England.

- **Coastal Route 1:** Drive from Portland to Freeport for scenic ocean views and charming small towns.
- **Cape Elizabeth Loop:** A short drive from Portland, this route takes you to iconic landmarks like Portland Head Light and Two Lights State Park.
- **Sebago Lake Drive:** Head inland to this stunning lake, ideal for a relaxing day trip.

**Contact:** Maine Tourism Bureau | (888) 624-6345 | visitmaine.com

## BIKING-FRIENDLY PUBLIC TRANSPORTATION

Travelers combining biking with public transit will love Portland's bike-friendly policies.

- **METRO Buses:** Equipped with bike racks on the front for easy loading.
- **Casco Bay Lines:** Allows bikes on ferries for a small fee ($6 round trip to Peaks Island).
- **Train Travel:** Amtrak's Downeaster allows bike transport with prior reservation.

---

**Insider Tip:** Combining biking and public transit is the easiest way to explore the islands or nearby towns without worrying about parking.

---

## MAKING THE MOST OF YOUR MOBILITY OPTIONS

Whether you prefer walking Portland's charming streets, biking along scenic trails, or zipping across the water by ferry, there's an option to match every pace and style. Portland's transportation network isn't just functional—it's an integral part of experiencing the city.

Now that you know how to navigate Portland with ease, your journey is ready to unfold. Whether you're planning a scenic drive to coastal gems, hopping on a ferry to an island getaway, or enjoying a leisurely walk downtown, the adventure lies not just in the destinations but in the way you move through the city. In the next section, we'll wrap up this guide with essential resources and tips to make your Portland experience unforgettable.

Planning a trip to Portland is part of the adventure. Whether it's deciding what to pack, setting a budget, or ensuring you have the resources for a safe and accessible journey, a little preparation goes a long way. This section provides the essential information to make your Portland experience seamless and enjoyable, leaving you free to focus on creating unforgettable memories.

# 29

# PACKING FOR PORTLAND

Packing for Portland is like preparing for a treasure hunt—you'll encounter historic streets, rugged coastlines, and vibrant food scenes, each with their own unique demands. With the right gear, you'll be ready to embrace every part of your adventure.

## SEASONAL ESSENTIALS

### Spring and Fall:

Portland's spring and fall weather is a mix of crisp mornings, warm afternoons, and cool evenings. Versatility is key.

**What to Pack**:

- Moisture-wicking base layers
- Mid-layers like fleece or sweaters for warmth
- A weather-resistant jacket to handle wind and rain
- Lightweight scarf or hat for extra comfort

### Summer:

Maine's summer days are warm and breezy, with cooler evenings by the water.

**What to Pack**:

- Light clothing such as shorts, tank tops, and sundresses
- A light sweater or jacket for evening strolls
- Sunglasses and sunscreen for sunny days

*Winter:*

Snowy streets and frosty mornings make winter an enchanting time to visit Portland—but preparation is crucial.

**What to Pack**:

- A heavy coat or parka
- Insulated boots with good traction
- Thermal base layers, gloves, a hat, and a scarf

## WALKING SHOES

Portland's cobblestone streets and nature trails demand the right footwear:

- **Old Port**: Sneakers or casual walking shoes with good arch support for exploring cobblestones.
- **Trails and Parks**: Lightweight hiking shoes or sturdy sneakers with traction for trails like the Eastern Promenade or Fore River Sanctuary.
- **Weather-Ready**: Waterproof shoes for rainy days or wet trails.

## WEATHER GEAR

Portland's maritime climate is as unpredictable as it is charming.

- **Rain Jacket**: A packable, breathable rain jacket with a hood for hands-free exploring.
- **Umbrella**: A compact, wind-resistant umbrella for rainy days.
- **Accessories**: A wide-brim hat for summer or a beanie for winter.

## ADDITIONAL MUST-HAVES

- **Daypack**: A lightweight backpack for carrying water, snacks, and your rain jacket.
- **Reusable Water Bottle**: Stay hydrated while exploring outdoor attractions.
- **Binoculars**: Perfect for birdwatching at Mackworth Island or spotting seals at Portland Head Light.
- **Portable Charger**: Keep devices charged for photos and navigation.
- **Camera or Smartphone**: Portland's landmarks—from the cobblestone streets to Portland Head Light—are photo-worthy.

## TAILORED PACKING TIPS FOR ALL TRAVELERS

- **Families**: Bring layers for kids to adapt to changing weather, as well as compact snacks and activities for downtime.
- **Solo Travelers**: Pack lightweight, versatile items to keep your bag manageable while staying ready for any adventure.
- **Romantic Getaways**: Include cozy scarves or wraps to share during sunset cruises or evening walks.

Packing thoughtfully ensures you're prepared to experience everything Portland has to offer. From the vibrant streets of the Old Port to the scenic trails along the coastline, your adventure awaits. With the right layers, weather-appropriate gear, and a spirit of exploration, you'll make unforgettable memories in Maine's coastal gem.

# 30

# BUDGETING YOUR TRIP

Portland is more than a destination; it's an experience tailored to every traveler. Whether you're savoring a lobster roll on a shoestring budget or indulging in waterfront fine dining, understanding how to budget will ensure you make the most of your visit.

## ACCOMMODATIONS

- **Budget-Friendly ($-$$)**: Hostels, motels, and vacation rentals outside downtown range from $80–$150 per night. Check South Portland or Westbrook for affordable yet accessible options.
- **Mid-Range ($$-$$$)**: Boutique hotels and charming B&Bs in the Old Port district typically cost $150–$300 per night.
- **Luxury ($$$$)**: Upscale waterfront hotels, like **Portland Harbor Hotel**, range from $300–$500+ per night, especially during peak season.

**Tips for Savings:**

- Visit during the off-season (late fall through early spring) for significantly lower rates.
- Use travel apps like **HotelTonight** for last-minute deals.
- If traveling in a group, consider splitting costs on vacation rentals.

## FOOD AND DRINKS

Portland's culinary scene caters to all budgets.

- **Casual Eats ($10–$30)**: Food trucks like **Bite Into Maine** and casual spots like **Otto Pizza** offer affordable, high-quality meals.
- **Mid-Range Dining ($30–$50)**: Local favorites like **Central Provisions** or **Fore Street** balance cost with exceptional flavors.
- **Fine Dining ($50–$100+)**: Iconic spots like **Hugo's** or **Solo Italiano** offer indulgent experiences worth the splurge.

**Tips for Savings**:

- Look for happy hours with discounted drinks and small plates at spots like **The Highroller Lobster Co.**
- Visit the **Portland Farmers' Market** for fresh produce and budget-friendly snacks.
- Share plates or opt for prix-fixe menus at high-end restaurants.

## ACTIVITIES AND ENTERTAINMENT

Portland offers a mix of free, mid-range, and luxury activities.

- **Free**: Explore the **Eastern Promenade**, stroll through the **Old Port**, or enjoy public beaches.
- **Mid-Range ($20–$50)**: Guided tours, brewery visits, or wildlife tours offer great value.

- **Luxury ($100–$250)**: Private sailing charters or exclusive food tastings provide unforgettable experiences.

**Tips for Savings**:

- Check for free museum admission days or donation-based tours.
- Combine free activities with one or two paid experiences to balance costs.
- Look for package deals, like brewery tours with tastings or historical walking tour bundles.

## SAMPLE BUDGET

Here's a breakdown of a daily budget for a single traveler:

- **Budget Traveler ($120–$150/day)**: Stay in a hostel or vacation rental, eat at food trucks, and enjoy free attractions like the Eastern Promenade.
- **Mid-Range Traveler ($200–$300/day)**: Stay in a boutique hotel, dine at mid-range restaurants, and include one paid activity.
- **Luxury Traveler ($400+/day)**: Stay in a luxury hotel, savor fine dining, and indulge in exclusive experiences like private tours.

Portland offers unforgettable experiences for every budget. Whether you're enjoying free trails, food truck delights, or Michelin-quality meals, thoughtful planning ensures every dollar spent is well worth it. With the right mix of savings and indulgences, Portland promises to leave you with memories that far outweigh the cost.

## 31

# SAFETY AND ACCESSIBILITY

Portland is a welcoming, inclusive city that invites everyone to enjoy its charm, but a little preparation can go a long way in ensuring a smooth trip. Whether navigating cobblestone streets or planning adaptive outdoor activities, these tips will help you explore with confidence.

## DRESSING FOR THE WEATHER

- **Spring & Fall**: Layer up to handle unpredictable coastal weather. Moisture-wicking base layers, fleece or sweaters, and waterproof jackets are must-haves.
- **Summer**: Pack lightweight, breathable clothing along with sunscreen, sunglasses, and a wide-brimmed hat to protect against UV rays.
- **Winter**: Insulated coats, boots with good traction, gloves, and hats are essential. Microspikes can make icy trails safer for adventurous visitors.

## FOOTWEAR

- **Cobblestone Streets**: Choose sturdy walking shoes with good arch support.
- **Trails and Parks**: Lightweight hiking boots or sneakers with traction are ideal for the Eastern Promenade or Fore River Sanctuary.
- **Weather-Ready**: Waterproof footwear is a smart choice for rainy days.

## TRANSPORTATION SAFETY

- Use rideshare apps like **Uber** and **Lyft** for stress-free travel during evenings out.
- Portland's public transit, including the METRO buses, is reliable and affordable. Plan ahead by checking schedules for buses and ferries.

## ALCOHOL AND FOOD SAFETY

- Sample Portland's craft beverages responsibly; many breweries offer non-alcoholic options.
- Communicate dietary restrictions to restaurants—Portland's culinary scene is known for being accommodating.

## GENERAL SAFETY TIPS

- Keep valuables secure in crowded areas like the Old Port or the farmers' markets.
- Solo travelers should share their itinerary with someone back home.
- Stick to marked trails during outdoor activities and carry a fully charged phone.

## ACCESSIBILITY RESOURCES

Portland is dedicated to creating an inclusive experience for travelers of all abilities.

### *Accessible Attractions*

- **Portland Museum of Art** (7 Congress Square): Fully wheelchair-accessible with elevators, accessible restrooms, and wheelchairs available for use.
- **Eastern Promenade Trail**: A scenic waterfront path that's paved and wheelchair-friendly.
- **Casco Bay Lines Ferry Terminal** (56 Commercial St.): Offers accessible boarding and facilities for island exploration.

### *Dining and Breweries*

- Many restaurants, like **Eventide Oyster Co.** and **Fore Street**, provide step-free access and spacious seating.
- Breweries like **Allagash Brewing Company** (50 Industrial Way) feature ramps, accessible restrooms, and large tasting rooms.

### *Outdoor Activities*

- **Adaptive Kayaking and Paddleboarding**: Offered by local organizations for exploring Casco Bay.
- **Back Cove Trail**: A flat, wheelchair-accessible loop with stunning bay views.

### *Transportation*

- **Greater Portland METRO Buses**: Equipped with wheelchair lifts and priority seating.
- **Accessible Parking**: Available throughout the city, especially near major attractions like the Old Port and Deering Oaks Park.

### *Additional Accessibility Tips*

- **Plan Ahead**: Research accommodations, attractions, and transportation for accessibility. Call ahead to confirm specific needs, like accessible seating or ferry boarding protocols.
- **Bring Necessary Equipment**: Pack backups for mobility aids, such as extra batteries for electric wheelchairs or umbrellas for unexpected weather.
- **Seek Local Assistance**: Visit Portland's tourism offices or contact visitor centers for real-time accessibility updates.

Portland is a destination that truly embraces all visitors, offering inclusive attractions, adaptive outdoor adventures, and thoughtful accessibility features. Whether you're navigating historic streets, savoring fresh seafood, or exploring scenic trails, a little preparation ensures your experience will be seamless and unforgettable.

## 32

# USEFUL CONTACTS

Whether you're planning your itinerary or navigating a surprise, having the right resources at your fingertips can make all the difference. This chapter provides a comprehensive list of emergency numbers, visitor centers, and apps to keep your Portland adventure smooth and stress-free.

## EMERGENCY NUMBERS

- **Emergency (Police, Fire, Medical)**: Dial 911 for immediate assistance.
- **Non-Emergency Police Line**: (207) 874-8575 (Portland Police Department).

## MEDICAL SERVICES

- **Maine Medical Center**: 22 Bramhall St., Portland, ME 04102 | (207) 662-0111.
- **Northern Light Mercy Hospital**: 175 Fore River Pkwy, Portland, ME 04102 | (207) 879-3000.

- **Urgent Dental Needs**: Maine Emergency Dental Clinic |
  (207) 780-2868.

## VISITOR CENTERS

Visitor centers are your go-to spots for local advice, maps, and personalized recommendations.

### Greater Portland Visitor Information Center

- **Location**: 14 Ocean Gateway Pier, Portland, ME 04101.
- **Phone**: (207) 772-5800.
- **Hours**: Open daily (hours vary seasonally).
- **Services**: Maps, brochures, event calendars, and tailored recommendations for attractions, dining, and activities.

### Maine Visitor Information Center (Freeport)

- **Location**: 95 Main St., Freeport, ME 04032.
- **Phone**: (207) 865-1212.
- **Services**: Advice on excursions, Freeport shopping, and outdoor activities.

### Casco Bay Lines Terminal Information Desk

- **Location**: 56 Commercial St., Portland, ME 04101.
- **Phone**: (207) 774-7871.
- **Services**: Ferry schedules, island activity tips, and waterfront attractions guidance.

## HELPFUL APPS

Take the guesswork out of exploring Portland with these essential apps:

### For Planning and Navigation

- **Visit Portland App**: Comprehensive guide to attractions, events, restaurants, and shopping.
- **Google Maps**: Reliable for walking, biking, and public transit schedules.

## For Foodies

- **Yelp**: Reviews and ratings for restaurants and cafes.
- **Resy/OpenTable**: Book reservations at top eateries.

## For Outdoor Enthusiasts

- **AllTrails**: Discover hiking and biking trails.
- **AccuWeather**: Stay updated on Portland's unpredictable weather.

## For Craft Beverage Lovers

- **Untappd**: Locate and review local breweries.
- **Distiller**: Recommendations for distilleries and spirits nearby.

## For Transportation

- **Lyft/Uber**: Ride-share options to explore Portland without a car.
- **Casco Bay Lines App**: Ferry schedules and ticket information for island adventures.

## EXPLORING BEYOND PORTLAND

If venturing to nearby towns or scenic spots, keep these resources handy:

- **Maine State Parks Information Line**: (207) 287-3200.
- **Acadia National Park Visitor Center**: (207) 288-3338.

## TAILORED ADVICE FOR ALL TRAVELERS

- **For Families**: Check visitor centers for kid-friendly activities like museums or seasonal events.
- **For Solo Travelers**: Use apps like AllTrails or Untappd to find scenic trails or cozy tasting rooms.
- **For Couples**: Ask visitor center staff for romantic spots like sunset viewpoints or intimate dining options.

With these resources in hand, you're ready to navigate Portland's vibrant energy with ease and confidence. From discovering hidden gems to planning day trips, the tools and tips here ensure that your Portland adventure will be as organized as it is unforgettable.

# CONCLUSION: YOUR PORTLAND ADVENTURE AWAITS

## REFLECTING ON PORTLAND'S CHARM

There's something undeniably magical about Portland, Maine. Perhaps it's the way the salty sea air mingles with the aroma of freshly baked bread from local bakeries or how the city's cobblestone streets whisper stories of its rich maritime history. Portland isn't just a destination; it's an experience that lingers long after you've returned home.

This coastal gem offers a perfect balance of old-world charm and modern vibrancy. Whether you've explored the historic Old Port, gazed at the iconic Portland Head Light, or indulged in a culinary journey through the city's award-winning restaurants, every moment in Portland feels like a memory in the making.

For history buffs, Portland provides a glimpse into its maritime legacy, from the tales of Fort Gorges to the hidden treasures of the Portland Observatory. Foodies discover a world-class culinary scene, blending traditional New England flavors with bold, innovative cuisine. Outdoor enthusiasts marvel at the city's natural beauty, from the serene Casco Bay islands to the vibrant foliage of autumn trails.

What makes Portland truly special, though, is its heart: the people. From friendly shop owners to passionate chefs and welcoming locals, the city radiates a warmth that feels like home. Whether this was your first visit or a return trip, Portland's charm has a way of making every traveler feel like a part of its story.

## ENCOURAGING READER ENGAGEMENT

Your journey through Portland doesn't end when you leave. In fact, it's just beginning. We encourage you to take the stories, tips, and hidden gems from this guide and make them your own. Whether you discovered a new favorite lobster roll spot or found serenity on a lesser-known trail, we'd love to hear about your experiences.

## SHARE YOUR STORY

Travel is about connection, and your perspective can inspire future visitors to explore Portland in their own way. Share your favorite moments, hidden finds, or must-visit spots on social media using the hashtag **#PortlandYourWay**. Your insights could help a fellow traveler uncover a new adventure or try a dish they might have otherwise missed.

## GET INVOLVED

Portland thrives because of its community, and visitors are part of that story. Support local businesses, attend events, and leave reviews for your favorite spots to help the city continue to grow and thrive. Whether it's a family-owned café or a local artist's gallery, your engagement keeps Portland's creative spirit alive.

## STAY CONNECTED

The beauty of Portland is that there's always more to discover. Join mailing lists for seasonal events, follow Portland's tourism accounts, or plan a return visit during a different season. Each trip offers a new perspective and fresh memories.

Portland isn't just a place you visit—it's a place you feel. Its beauty lies in the layers: the history beneath your feet, the flavors on your plate, and the stories that unfold with every step. As you close this guide and reflect on your journey, know that Portland is always here, ready to welcome you back.

Until then, we hope this book inspires you to seek out new adventures, savor the unexpected, and embrace the spirit of exploration. Thank you for letting us be part of your Portland story—now go write the next chapter.

# THANK YOU DEAR READER

Hey there!

I just wanted to say a big thank you for diving into my book! It truly means so much to me that you enjoyed it all the way through. 🩶

I would love to hear what you thought! Your feedback, whether it's what you loved or things that could be better, really helps me and other readers.

If you could spare a few minutes to leave a review, that would be amazing! You can share it on Amazon, Goodreads, or wherever you picked up the book.

Thanks again for your support! Getting to connect with readers like you makes writing such a joy.

Take care, and happy reading!

– Kimberly

# APPENDICES: CALENDAR OF EVENTS – ANNUAL FESTIVALS AND SEASONAL ACTIVITIES

## JANUARY

### • Portland On Tap

*When*: Mid-January

*Where*: Portland, ME

*What*: Beer festival featuring samples from over 60 breweries, live music, and food vendors.

*Website*: www.portlandontap.com

## FEBRUARY

### • Maine Restaurant Week

*When*: Late February–Early March

*Where*: Statewide, including Portland

*What*: Culinary celebration with special prix fixe menus at participating restaurants.

*Website*: www.mainerestaurantweek.com

## MARCH

### • **Maine Flower Show**

*When*: Late March/Early April

*Where*: Brick South at Thompson's Point, Portland, ME

*What*: Stunning floral displays, gardening workshops, and landscaping exhibits.

*Website*: maineflowershow.com

### • **Portland Museum of Art Spring Exhibitions**

*When*: March–May

*Where*: Portland Museum of Art, 7 Congress Square, Portland

*What*: Seasonal exhibits featuring contemporary and classic art from regional and global artists.

*Website*: www.portlandmuseum.org

## APRIL

### • **Portland Wine Week**

*When*: Late April

*Where*: Various venues in Portland

*What*: Wine tastings, pairing dinners, and educational seminars for wine enthusiasts.

*Website*: www.portlandwineweek.me

## MAY

### • **Spring Waterfront Cruises**

*When*: May

*Where*: Casco Bay Lines Terminal, 56 Commercial St., Portland

*What*: Scenic harbor cruises celebrating the arrival of warmer weather and emerging coastal wildlife.

• **Maine Coast Marathon**

*When*: Mid-May

*Where*: Kennebunk to Biddeford, ME

*What*: Scenic marathon along the beautiful Maine coastline.

*Website*: www.mainecoast262.com

## JUNE

• **Old Port Festival** *(Check local updates for alternatives)*

*When*: Early June

*Where*: Old Port District, Portland

*What*: Live music, food vendors, and street performers in a vibrant day-long festival.

*Website*: www.portlandmaine.com/old-port-festival

• **Portland Beer Week**

*When*: Late June–Early July

*Where*: Breweries across Portland

*What*: A celebration of craft beer with tastings, brewery tours, and exclusive pairing events.

## JULY

• **Yarmouth Clam Festival**

*When*: Mid-July

*Where*: Yarmouth, ME

*What*: Parades, clam shucking contests, and artisan crafts celebrate Maine's seafood heritage.

*Website*: www.clamfestival.com

## • Maine Brewers' Guild Summer Session

*When*: Late July

*Where*: Portland, ME

*What*: A gathering of Maine's craft brewers for tastings and live music.

*Website*: www.mainebrewersguild.org

## AUGUST

## • Maine Lobster Festival

*When*: Late July/Early August

*Where*: Rockland, ME (about 90 minutes from Portland)

*What*: Celebrate Maine's lobster industry with fresh seafood, cooking contests, and live music.

*Website*: www.mainelobsterfestival.com

## • St. Peter's Italian Bazaar

*When*: Mid-August

*Where*: Portland, ME

*What*: A cultural festival celebrating Italian heritage with food, music, and traditions.

*Website*: www.facebook.com/StPetersItalianBazaar

## SEPTEMBER

• **Common Ground Country Fair**

*When*: Late September

*Where*: Unity, ME

*What*: Agricultural fair focused on organic farming and sustainability.

*Website*: www.mofga.org/the-fair

• **Fall Foliage Exploration**

*When*: September–October

*Where*: Eastern Promenade, Back Cove, and nearby state parks

*What*: Immerse yourself in Maine's vibrant fall colors with hikes and scenic drives.

*Tip*: Use the Maine Foliage Tracker to find peak foliage.

## OCTOBER

• **Harvest on the Harbor**

*When*: Late October

*Where*: Various venues in Portland

*What*: Multi-day culinary event featuring farm-to-table pairings and local chefs.

*Website*: www.harvestontheharbor.com

• **Portland Film Festival**

*When*: October

*Where*: Various theaters in Portland

*What*: Independent films, documentaries, and filmmaker panels.

## NOVEMBER

### • Monument Square Tree Lighting

*When*: Late November/Early December

*Where*: Monument Square, Portland

*What*: Festive holiday kickoff with music, hot cocoa, and twinkling lights.

## DECEMBER

### • Portland Harbor Christmas Boat Parade of Lights

*When*: Early December

*Where*: Portland Harbor

*What*: Festive boats decorated with holiday lights.

*Website*: www.portlandmaine.com/boat-parade-of-lights

### • Ice Skating at Thompson's Point Rink

*When*: December–February

*Where*: 10 Thompson's Point, Portland

*What*: Outdoor skating with Fore River views. Rentals available.

### • Kennebunkport Christmas Prelude

*When*: Early December

*Where*: Kennebunkport, ME

*What*: Holiday celebration with parades, tree lightings, and seasonal festivities.

*Website*: www.christmasprelude.com

## YEAR-ROUND

### • Farmers' Markets

*When*: Year-round (Seasonal Locations)

*Where*: Deering Oaks Park in summer; 631 Stevens Ave in winter

*What*: Fresh produce, artisan goods, and local treats.

### • First Friday Art Walk

*When*: First Friday of each month

*Where*: Downtown Portland galleries and studios

*What*: A free event with art exhibits, live music, and community gatherings.

Kimberly Burk Cordova is an accomplished author, entrepreneur, and cultural enthusiast whose passion for exploration and storytelling shines through her work. As the founder of Cordova Consulting, Kimberly has dedicated her career to leadership development, strategic business solutions, and personal growth, bringing over three decades of experience in IT and technology to her clients. Her journey, however, extends far beyond boardrooms and digital transformations.

A former resident of Portland, Maine, Kimberly fell in love with the city's charm, history, and vibrant community during her time living there with her daughter Channa and son-in-law Stephen. While Stephen worked at the shipyard in nearby Kittery, Kimberly immersed herself in the richness of Portland's neighborhoods, its culinary wonders, and its breathtaking coastline. Portland became more than a place she called home—it became a city she cherished, and her love for it is infused throughout the pages of this book.

Now residing in Santa Fe, New Mexico, Kimberly draws inspiration from the region's rich artistic heritage and awe-inspiring landscapes. Her dual connection to Maine's rugged beauty and New Mexico's vibrant culture informs her storytelling, making her work a heartfelt tribute to the places and people that have shaped her life.

Kimberly's love of travel and cultural exploration has taken her across the globe, but Portland holds a special place in her heart. In this guide, she shares her intimate knowledge of the city, weaving her experiences as a resident with her trademark warmth and engaging storytelling. Whether it's recounting her strolls through the West End's cobblestone streets or the joy of exploring Portland's James Beard

Award-winning restaurants with Channa and Stephen, Kimberly brings Portland to life with authenticity and affection.

Beyond her professional accomplishments, Kimberly's life is enriched by her close-knit family. She shares her journey with her husband, Greg, and treasures the moments she spends with her grandchildren, Vera and Tillman, who bring endless light and laughter to her days. Her family's experiences in Portland have left an indelible mark, shaping the perspectives she shares in her writing.

Through Cordova Consulting, Kimberly offers a diverse range of books, workshops, and resources that reflect her love for leadership, growth, travel, and storytelling. Her work resonates with readers and clients alike, inviting them to explore, reflect, and find inspiration in life's many journeys.

Kimberly's writing is a testament to her belief in the transformative power of stories. Whether she's exploring leadership, resilience, or the unique charm of Portland, she invites her readers to join her in uncovering the beauty and richness of life. Dive into Kimberly's world, and let her passion for connection, culture, and discovery guide your own adventure.

amazon.com/author/kimberlycordova

goodreads.com/kbcordova

youtube.com/@CordovaConsulting

facebook.com/CordovaCons

linkedin.com/in/kimberlyburk

tiktok.com/@kimberlyburkcordova

# ALSO BY KIMBERLY BURK CORDOVA

## LEADERSHIP SERIES

- Turning Chaos into Gold: The Alchemy of Women's Leadership
- The Emotional Intelligence Advantage: Transform Your Life, Relationships, and Career
- The Emotional Intelligence Advantage: Transform Your Life, Relationships, and Career

## TRAVEL SERIES

- Santa Fe Uncovered: A Local's Insight into the Heart of New Mexico
- Santa Fe: A Local's Enchanting Journey Through the City Different
- Denver Dossier: Themed Adventures for Every Traveler
- Portland Your Way: A Guide for Every Traveler, Style, and Season in Portland, Maine

## EMPOWERING SMALL BUSINESSES SERIES

- Artificial Intelligence Unleashed: An Entrepreneur's Guide to Innovation

- Augmented and Virtual Reality: Unlocking Business Potential for Entrepreneurs
- Cybersecurity for Entrepreneurs: Safeguarding Your Business from Online Threats
- The Entrepreneur's Edge: A 3-Book Compilation on AI, Cybersecurity, and AR/VR

# ALSO BY PUBLISHER CORDOVA CONSULTING

## Author - Eliza Hawthorne

## SHADOWS OF THE PAST SERIES

- The Vanishing Heiress: The Unsolved Disappearance of Dorothy Arnold
- The Silent Witness: The Unsolved Murder of Mary Rogers
- Whispers from the Murder Farm: The Case of Belle Gunness: Inside the Mind of America's Darkest Femme Fatale

## SHADOWS OF THE PAST BOX SETS

- THE VANISHING ACT: UNSOLVED CASES OF AMERICA'S MOST MYSTERIOUS WOMEN: SHADOWS OF THE PAST: THE FIRST TRILOGY COLLECTION